FINDING ORDER IN DISORDER

A BIPOLAR MEMOIR

FINDING ORDER IN DISORDER

A BIPOLAR MEMOIR

Ishaa Vinod Chopra

Om Books International

First published in 2024 by

Om Books International

Corporate & Editorial Office
A-12, Sector 64, Noida 201 301
Uttar Pradesh, India
Phone: +91 120 477 4100
Email: editorial@ombooks.com
Website: www.ombooksinternational.com

Sales Office
107, Ansari Road, Darya Ganj,
New Delhi 110 002, India
Phone: +91 11 4000 9000
Email: sales@ombooks.com
Website: www.ombooks.com

ISBN: 978-93-94547-10-0

Printed in India

10 9 8 7 6 5 4 3 2 1

For my parents, Vinod and Shabnam

Dedicated to the memory of my beloved uncle, Vir Papa...
Your memory is a blessing...

Am I the observer, or the bird that takes flight into the horizon? Am I a follower seated amongst the crowd, or am I a leader who takes a step forward and sets herself free? Whoever I maybe, I fit perfectly into this chaotic universe, with its unbalanced beauty…

I am forever finding order in disorder.

Contents

Introduction

The primary reason for writing this book is that there is a need to create more awareness about mental health issues. Although mental health literacy is greater in Western societies, conversations are not as open as they need to be. In India, they barely exist, especially in rural regions. This must change. Although now depression is being openly talked about to some extent, we largely live in the dark on the topic of mental health. The condition I have been diagnosed with, bipolar disorder, is not known to many. I know this because one of the rehabs I resided at in India had patients who were coping primarily with drug addiction, gambling and alcoholism, and not so much with mood disorders. Self-created and manmade problems are often thought of as 'real' issues, but what about the ones that people are born with due to their genes? It surely should be possible for us to talk about these problems, too, openly and for us to deal with them, not just as individuals but as a society.

I think my life and all the struggles would have been in vain if I did not write this book. In my short life so far, my family has been involved with all the major decisions I took as I moved from one continent to the other. I have had to adapt and undergo several changes in a short period of time. Dividing my time between India, Germany and Canada resulted in an instability that culminated with the manifestation of my bipolar episodes. Moving constantly has also hampered my mental well-being in other ways. I might have benefitted by having a strong social circle if I had stayed in one place. Having an early marriage further exposed me to many unpleasant situations. My then husband almost broke my back in two. The experience was truly traumatic, especially at the young age of twenty-three. That I kept my family unaware of it was, in hindsight, something that only made it worse for me. It was emotionally scarring, as well as physically damning. But all these experiences have chiselled my character. Being a Kathak and Latin dance artist has helped me cope with many challenges in the past, and continues to give me a deeper insight into my ever-evolving identity.

Writing this book has given me an opportunity to put down my thoughts about life. This could have been a simple account, an analysis or an interpretation, but I have also in a way developed a philosophy, as it were. While I know I have a lot more to learn and this is just the beginning, I still want to share my experiences with the world, especially with those who have encountered mental health conditions in some way or the other in their life. I want to join those who are striving to normalize conversations around mental health. It is not only okay to speak about it, but also beneficial. We can all learn from each other's mistakes and insights. But I want to go one step further and tell you why these experiences enrich our life. By offering readers a glimpse of my hospital stays, I hope you too can reimagine hospitals as places of healing, learning and hope.

This book has also given me the opportunity to share my thoughts on domestic violence and foreground how it can sometimes be worse for those with mental health conditions. It was a sensitive topic, but as a survivor of violence and abuse, I consider it my duty to share my experience for the sake of other survivors and their friends and families, who are affected by it on a daily basis. I hope that my efforts to speak about it will not go in vain and people will continue to find ways to prevent and possibly even end domestic violence against women the world over.

My heart goes out to all the people who are diagnosed with mental health conditions, so I strive to fight the stigma associated with such illnesses through this book. In India, especially, it is difficult to find families who are accepting of these conditions, but the stigma exists in workplaces in the West as well. Many people who are diagnosed with bipolar disorder in particular prefer to hide their condition for this reason. The threat of rejection emanating from our society instills fear in minorities of all kinds.

The fear and stigma affect people like me adversely in more ways than one. Societal pressure makes it challenging for those with mental health conditions to maintain a healthy lifestyle, for instance. Besides, practices common in mainstream culture, such as drugs, alcohol and gambling, prevent them from thriving, create obstacles for them and make things worse as they fall through the cracks.

In addition to the stigma and the pressure, once a person is diagnosed with a condition, they are often denied all control on account of it. Having been through multiple hospitalizations, especially in rehabs, in both the East and West, I have overcome many hurdles and have had to brave many challenges related to this. On some occasions I was tied down to a bed, or sent into isolation, and sometimes I even had memory lapses due to the high dosage of medication. Several medications had their side effects and I, unfortunately, had no control over the choice of drugs; I often had to down a cocktail of drugs. In addition, the constant change of doctors did not aid the recovery process. Excessive reliance on medication alone is not recommended. Being constantly drowsy, as opposed to manic, is not the solution. It is, like they say, jumping from the frying pan into the fire. I therefore advocate for greater accessibility of counselling sessions, apart from nursing facilities and medication, but most importantly prioritizing the views of patients.

This book is also my endeavour to reach out to the families of people with mental health conditions. Patients need all the support they can get, especially from families. Families may support the individual in various ways, just like mine did all along my journey with this disorder—either by reaching out to a doctor, nurse or counsellor to help intervene, or, as in my case, by preventing the repercussions of domestic violence. There is no place for control.

The real catalyst that prompted me to complete this book was my mother's film *Unfinished*, her thesis on mental health. I had started writing my book before my mother began making the film, but it was the process in which the film was made that made me determined to write the book.

There were times when the way the film was made appeared rather unethical to me. My mother would often film me when I wasn't in the right state of mind. My brother Ishan too would film our daily life, its ups and downs. None of us probably realized the ramifications of this. It says a lot about our tenacity and willingness to confront everything we were experiencing that we went through with this. Thinking back, given our artistic inclinations, it isn't surprising that we adopted this approach. We were basically utilizing art as a means to cope with the same and achieve a catharsis of sorts.

I am not sure we were aware of or comprehended the results of doing this but none of us regret it. I must admit I was extremely nervous in the beginning. Was my mother taking advantage of my delicate state? What if she crossed the line between a mother and a filmmaker; when did one role end and the other begin? I had many doubts, especially because some interviews would trigger me, but I knew I had to dig deep to clean my mind space. I am sure the film was cathartic for my mother too. It helped her address the residues of bitter memories and pain which had made her relationship a difficult one.

Unfinished screened at film festivals pertaining to mental health, as well as at CILECT (Centre international de liaison des écoles de cinéma et de télévision or The International Association of Film and Television Schools) where it won the first prize for a student film. It was also screened at the Centre for Addiction and Mental Health (CAMH), where I also happened to be treated.

After the film was made and screened at various festivals, I was determined to complete the book in response to the experience I had working with my mother. *Finding Order in Disorder* is the result of that very reaction and my own cathartic process. It taught me that whether or not you have a mental health disability, it is important to own your feelings, and sort them. The only way to throw out garbage and let go is to sort through it and eventually detach yourself from it in a positive manner.

Finally, art in any form—a film, a book, a piece of music, a painting—relieves us of the pain that we experience, or perhaps gives us answers to many questions, and solutions to various problems. I truly believe that dance, art and yoga are therapeutic activities. The process of painting, while in the hospital, helped channel my surplus energy and calmed me down. While completing my early childhood education at George Brown College, Toronto, I learnt how art is beneficial not just for those with mental health issues, but a great tool for children to develop an overall sense of emotional regulation. Art helps to gain better control over one's behaviour and improves one's ability to concentrate.

I hope you enjoy reading *Finding Order in Disorder*. I do not use difficult language to communicate, and try to speak my truth as honestly as I can. Although I believe in what I have said in this book, I still struggle to follow everything. I would like to end the beginning of my memoir with a quote by Kahlil Gibran: 'Out of suffering have emerged the strongest souls; the most massive characters are seared with scars.'

1

Early Years

The Distant Rumbling of Thunder

I was a year old when my mother left me to pursue film studies in Pune. I spent numerous hours with my maternal grandmother. We used to go out and roam the city, eating good food and viewing as many movies as we could at Gaiety-Galaxy, one of the few independent local cinemas to still survive in Mumbai. My grandmother tried her best to provide me with all the love she could and helped me cope with my mother's absence.

I wish I could recall more of my early years with my parents besides the fact that I found myself being moved from one home to another constantly due to their separation. I spent most of my vacations travelling up and down Mumbai, dividing my time between my parents.

The experiences that our parents and grandparents live through get passed down to us by word of mouth, behaviours and many other invisible ways. Intergenerational trauma is a concept that is now spoken of openly. However, until we look closely into what it might mean for us in the long run, it will be difficult to understand its effects on our adult lives. Therefore, it is challenging to pinpoint it, define it and address it. It is so engrained in our every thought, behaviour and feelings that we are oblivious to the fact that something somewhere that took place a long time ago is dictating our destinies. This is why it is important to analyse and magnify using our mind's looking glass the aspects of a personality that may not be so desirable but have been passed on through the generations. We cannot change our genes, of course, but we can positively influence our environment and our relationships with our close ones through refined processes and actions.

When we talk about mental health, it is no doubt a concept which is infused with intergenerational trauma. For example, in my case, my mother and maternal grandmother both had issues with their marriages, and overall, the way they viewed men was influenced by what their own mother had taught them. This almost always worked against them. My paternal grandmother, whom we called Ma, was a smiling ball of energy. Whatever she might have gone through, we never saw her sad, and we used to look up to her in times of sorrow and joy. She held the entire family together. She had several children and was a grandma of many more. The relationship she shared with each one of her grandkids of all ages was remarkable. She took immense pleasure in cooking, especially the Kashmiri wazwan recipes, such as rogan josh, dum aloo and, of course, my all-time favourite, paneer kalia. Paneer kalia was always prepared when I visited Kalpana, the name of the flat where Ma resided with my uncle Vijay Papa and cousins Peru Didi and Vicky Bhaiya. I cherished each meal I shared with all of them and would later be grateful for the times I did get to create memories with each one of them.

On the other hand, even though I received large amounts of love from my maternal grandmother, her love was wrapped in misery, for there were many times she would break down and cry in front of us. These emotions balanced out with my paternal grandmother as she would provide us with enough smiles to last a lifetime. Having said this, I understand the way we act with our children is a direct result of our own lived experiences, and my nani did not have the privilege of experiencing many positive ones with her late husband, my nana-ji. So, her entire world view was influenced by those lived experiences and the eventual loss of her husband, when my mother was merely fourteen years old.

I had many complexes as a child. My parents divorced with mutual consent when I was only five, and after this I spent most of my time with my mother, who had sole custody of me. She was of course a single mother, and as far as I can recollect, it took its time to heal completely; this was but understandable.

As a matter of fact, my mother was also prone to mental health issues. She lost her father at the tender age of fourteen, which resulted in issues in her relationships with men. Perhaps she had married my father because he reminded her of my grandfather, for both were film-makers. While my grandfather worked primarily on documentary films, my father directed and produced mainstream feature films in Mumbai. Eventually, after a few years of a turbulent marriage, they took the difficult decision of leaving each other. By the time she became a mother, some parts of her past had seeped through her relationship with me. Today, I understand the dynamics of human relationships a little better to be able to take a more empathetic view of this.

When you are a child, some moments make an indelible impression on you. My mother loves me a lot, but I now feel that her ability to parent me initially was impacted by her difficulty in coping with her divorce.

My mother and I have always shared a strong bond of attachment and love riddled with conflict. While growing up, I did not get as much quality time to spend with my mother—or father, for that matter—until I moved to Canada at the age of twelve where I resided with my mother and stepfather. We lived quite harmoniously in Edmonton, Alberta. However, this was where my diagnosis of bipolar would eventually come to light. This impacted the relationship I shared with my mother. It was challenging for her to accept my disorder. Also difficult for her was coming to terms with the manner in which I behaved when I was sick, to differentiate between the person I was and how I came across when going through an 'episode'. My father grappled with the same problem initially. However, now everyone in my family is aware of what constitutes an illness as opposed to a personality.

In even the most normal circumstances, relationships between parents and children are fraught. Both look at their positions from their vantage points, excluding the other.

In my case, this was aggravated with my diagnosis. And it wasn't easy on my mother, who probably did not, in the days leading to and after my marriage, have the bandwidth to deal with what I was experiencing. However, when I fell sick a year after marriage, it was my mother who came running to the airport to receive me. She was always there to prevent a fall, although in some cases she could even have been the reason for the fall. But I don't want to blame anyone in my family since after a point, we must take responsibility for our own decisions and actions. Indulging in a blame game serves no purpose and is, in the end, self-defeating.

The diagram on Page 8, which I drew during my first bipolar episode, describes in more ways than one what I felt about my parents and their differences. Even in my sickness I would feel this keenly: My parents, both fiercely similar, had increasingly begun to repel each other, unlike opposite poles.

Despite everything, I know my family shielded me to the best extent they could.

After the divorce, my childhood was essentially spent in two boarding schools. The first one, St. Mary's, had me residing in a gloomy building with even gloomier wardens, Ms Samuel and Ms Henderson. I can still recall their facial features clearly. Ms Samuel used to express her resentment towards students by slapping them and twisting their ears. My grandma would bribe her with expensive gifts so she wouldn't hurt me as much, but despite this I remained a victim of abuse, as did the rest of my classmates. It was only much later that I mentioned

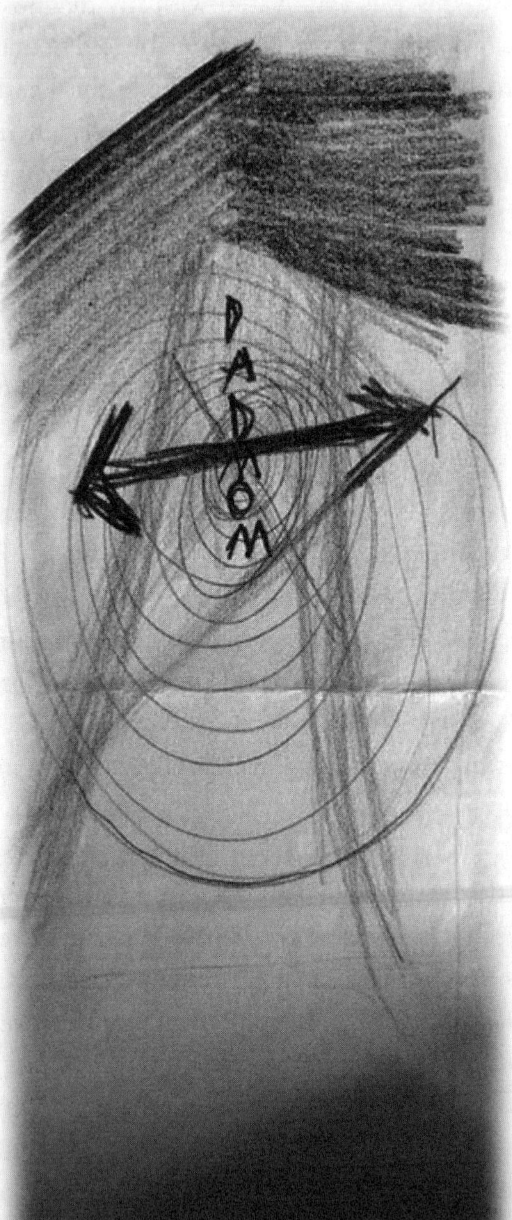
DAD
OM

these things to my mother. She spoke about it with my father who then ensured I was removed from St. Mary's. Eventually, the school shut down its boarding facility. When I learnt of this, I was ever so satisfied. No child should ever be exposed to such cruelty, especially in their early years.

The next boarding school I attended was run by the J. Krishnamurti foundation and it was named after the Sahyadri hill range where it was situated. This institution was a dream come true. They made us assume duties, such as washing our own clothes, encouraging us to begin to be independent, but we didn't mind.

The Sahyadri School campus had a small hill named Asthachal Hill. We used to climb it every evening at five to observe the sunset, watch the sun go down slowly but surely. The calming effect it had on all of us, including the hyper ones like me, was truly remarkable. These memories of my childhood will never fade away. Even today, when I feel too wired up, I like to be amidst nature to observe the setting sun.

We had an art room which had all forms of art on display, including batik and pottery. The art room was surrounded by cherry trees, and I loved to climb them with my friends to pick the fruit.

The Bhima River flows right through the Sahyadri range; we used to go for long treks there—sometimes getting bitten by scorpions—followed by a swim in the river. Other times we would go to Shambhu Hill, which had a beautiful temple;

after a long trek, we would say our prayers or merely wait for the priest to give us sweets (barfi).

Our mornings began with 'Geet Gunjan', where our tabla instructor, music teachers, sitar player, and senior students sang bhajans. We would all join in, following the lyrics from a book of devotional songs. Our music would reverberate through the entire auditorium and imbue us with positivity. Decades later, I am still reminded of that time, especially the melody of that music, which remains etched in my memory. Those graceful mornings spent at Sahyadri School laid the foundation for my interest in Indian classical dance and music. I was so deeply influenced that I would later go on to continue my education in performing arts with a degree in Kathak from Bharati Vidyapeeth, Pune, under the able guidance of Guru Pta Maneesha Sathe.

A year after I joined the school, my mother came in as a Hindi teacher, giving up a great job as a media consultant for a company, based out of Mumbai, so that she could spend more time with me. They say everything happens for a reason. Truly, her move was a blessing, as it was there that she met her present husband, my 'Abba', who was a music teacher in the school at the time. They have a son, my brother Ishan. I was thirteen years old when he was born.

My interest in children was ignited during the long hours I used to spend babysitting Ishan. I sang the Beatles' songs that Abba taught me to him and would cradle him to sleep. Sometimes, he would go to bed with me rather than my mom. Changing his diapers was another delightful task for me. My new-found passion included arranging his toys in a neat row for him so that he could engage himself with all his toys simultaneously.

My interest in early childhood education was inspired by the time I spent with my younger brother. Apart from the long hours I spent playing with him, I also found babysitting opportunities with other children in my community during these years.

After living for a few years in India and working at Dalhousie Public School, I moved back to Toronto to live with my brother Ishan, Abba and my mother. This is where my mother became increasingly involved in my care and support to the extent of basing her York University master's thesis in the form of a documentary, titled *Unfinished*, on mental health featuring me.

*

Another new relationship that I had to come to terms with early on in life was the one with my stepmother, Anu-mummy. I now believe that after my father's marriage with my mother ended, he married the sweetest woman to walk this planet. Unfortunately, this was not always how I saw her. At an early age, one of my aunts planted many negative seeds in my head to turn me against her. In addition to that, the negative portrayal of stepmothers in films and books also had its impact on me. Not to mention the attitude of my maternal grandma. She was simply being protective but ended up damaging the image of my stepmother for me.

However, many things that took place later revealed her true character to me (for instance, her reaction to my marriage; more on that in the next chapter). With time and also what I gathered from her talk and behaviour, I now know that she cares for my father's well-being, so both of us have the same interest at heart. And what could possibly be better than that?

Over time, I made peace with the idea of having another mother figure in my life. She always showered me with love and honest advice, and was always the best at choosing the perfect gifts for not only me, but the entire extended family.

This is a perfect example of how society engrains certain ideas and prejudices in our head, which tend to adversely impact our ability to make decisions independently, especially in the case of young, impressionable minds.

2

Teenage Years

The Cracks Begin to Show

'Not until we are lost do we begin to understand ourselves.'

—Henry David Thoreau

What is life we wonder?
It is a good thing to wonder.
It makes us human…
If we did not wonder and ask the question 'why', what then would life be?

I had my first bipolar episode at the age of sixteen. I feel there are reasons for every manifestation—whether it be in the body or mind—and it is important to understand and acknowledge the past in order to start healing. Once we look closely into why a certain event occurred, perhaps we can prevent a similar thing from recurring.

Just a few months before my thirteenth birthday, I shifted to Edmonton in Alberta, Canada, with my mother and stepfather. My stepbrother from my stepfather's previous marriage also joined us. My high-school experience was much like that of any other teenage immigrant. I faced a lot of racism. Sometimes I would get teased because of my colour and other times I would face rejection due to my strong Indian accent. I remember one incident clearly where some of my classmates left me a note in my locker clearly outlining how I smelt of Indian spices.

The Indian accent that I had was of course 'corrected' within a matter of a few months. I was so eager to fit in that I unconsciously or consciously changed my accent. I now know that it was the people perceiving my accent who have a problem in the way they view others. My accent wasn't the problem. But when I had newly shifted to Canada, to me, it seemed as if I was the one with the problem. (When I moved back to India six years later, I once again found myself adopting the Indian accent; however, I believe I now have some kind of a mix of the Indian and Canadian accents.)

Interestingly, all these years later I recall commenting on an Indian-origin classmate of mine something to the effect that she wasn't 'Indian' enough. The comment reached her soon enough and she confronted me about it. That is when I realized that both of us being South Asians, we were dealing with our own concoction of an identity crisis. I was trying to fit it seamlessly into the Canadian culture while she was questioning and perhaps trying to seek answers on what parts of her constituted her Indian identity and what that would eventually mean for the way she viewed herself, as well as how others perceived her. We both dealt with our own individually unique internal battles.

Once, my mother was making a documentary film (*Ishaa Journals*) about the immigrant youth experience. In an interview for the film, she asked a fifteen-year-old me, 'Do you think I fit in here?' I replied, 'I do not think you fit in here but you are doing a great job pretending.' I was basically projecting my own feelings about not fitting in well—this was the subtext of my response to my mother. Both of us were going through our own journeys as immigrants, and talking about it to each other made the journey easier for both.

*

Another event impacted me a lot around this time. A close friendship came to an end due to a baseless accusation made by some of my classmates.

I had two friends back then, Cayte Kim and Iman. Iman was easily carried away by what others thought of me and stopped talking to me in the wake of the rumour. But Cayte stayed by my side and attempted her best to balance her time between Iman and me. Later, I also ended up discovering a true friend in my classmate, Victoria Todhunter. She proved to be one of my best friends, shrugging off all the rumours and explaining to me that the reason I was targeted was that people were jealous of my beauty, my cocoa-brown skin and well-defined features. All that, coming from a Canadian who had lived in that country for generations, was music to my ears.

This is when I learnt that true friends stand by you no matter what the circumstances are or which part of the world they come from. And during tough times, when it seems like you have nothing to offer to the world, they see you through.

*

Looking back and comparing my experiences in India to those in Canada, I would like to focus briefly on the concept of space. As it is understood and practised in the West, many people there do not like to interfere with the private affairs of others. But we are a social species, which is to say we prosper when we are surrounded by our loved ones. From my experience, in urban Mumbai and my boarding school, Sahyadri, I feel that the concept of space is different in this part of the world. People hug each other regardless of gender and are to some extent 'touchy-feely' with the best of intentions. Hence, moving to the West had me in shock, as people there largely kept to themselves and lived their lives in isolation.

While there is definitely more awareness for mental health conditions in the West, which is probably why more people get diagnosed in that part of the world, there are still several gaps in treatment and recovery. Doctors are at times too quick to resort to medication as the only means of treatment. So, often, patients there are overmedicated. Many cannot afford therapy because it is expensive. It's a real tragedy because therapy is an immensely crucial aspect of mental health treatment alongside medication.

In India, the situation couldn't be worse; disorders are often pushed under the carpet and are therefore unreported due to the stigma associated with them. So much so that even patients who have been diagnosed rarely share or talk about their condition for fear of being ostracized. I was always very open about my condition despite this. In my case however, the family was supportive, and circumstances—my mother's remarriage, my stepfather's acceptance, resources and facilities for treatment—

panned out favourably for my move to Canada.

The Beginning of Bipolar

It all started when I was sixteen years of age. At the time, I was attending a Model United Nations camp in Banff, Alberta. When I returned home after two weeks, I did not get any sleep. I kept coming up with different theories for changing the world. My parents thought that perhaps I was on drugs, but later when the doctors conducted blood tests, they knew it was something else.

An important factor to take into account is that sometimes high altitudes can also cause and trigger an episode if the gene exists. This now seems to make sense because Banff is situated at a very high altitude.

Initially, I had what doctors would later label a 'full-blown mixed episode', wherein I experienced sleepless nights. I began to think that I wanted to make a big difference in the world. I had come up with what I called 'a theory of intentions'. The idea I harboured was that Albert Einstein as well as Adolf Hitler were both geniuses—one with benign intentions and the other with malevolent ones. I thought it was of great significance, but there was of course no way to put the theory to use. And there was no way to measure or predict an individual's 'intentions' anyway.

Here's a diagram of the theory I had drawn during this period.

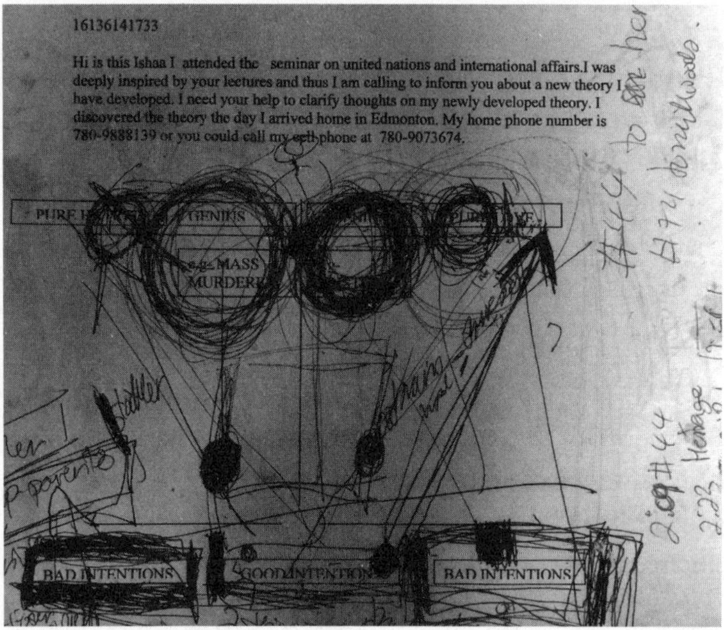

I have vivid memories of having heightened bodily sensations during this time. I was convinced that I was carrying God's child.

I had also just completed reading the Harry Potter series and could relate with Hermione's character the most. One time, when my mother was taking me to the hospital, I was convinced that I was being driven to Hogwarts where I would eventually be taught magic.

Having spent almost all of that year in hospital, I now think that in a way it was indeed a world of magic that I was going to be exposed to. I was on heavy medication. The doctors were trying to differentiate between schizo-affective disorder and bipolar. My theory now is that I was kept in hospital for a longer period of time so they could test as many medicines on me as they could—and my family wouldn't really get to know. I was perhaps a guinea pig, but I am happy to have been of some help to the medical society in my own way.

I do recognize that despite this, I was blessed to have been in Canada when I fell sick, for it did help us arrive at the correct diagnosis quickly. Besides, I have a good memory from this time as well—an incident that occurred towards the end of my stay there. A nurse gave me a list on the morning of the day of my discharge from the hospital. It is an extremely special list that I still have with me to this day. It included the names of many high achievers who have been diagnosed with bipolar disorder. I was amazed to find so many talented artists included in that list, from Vincent van Gogh to Jimi Hendrix.

That day, I walked out of the hospital feeling I could conquer the world. I knew that day that I was special or at least I convinced myself that I may be among the chosen ones. But this too is a characteristic of mania in my condition and, as I would come to realize later, these special feelings of being 'chosen', as good as they may feel, must be kept in check.

I now believe hardships come your way simply because God or the universal power believes you to be capable of handling them. It is also true that we all have our share of problems, so we should not undermine somebody else's problems by making comparisons. My father always says that there are only two real problems in this world: dire poverty and poor health; the rest are all created by us. If only we could gracefully accept this fact, we would be at peace with ourselves, the universe and the greater power.

*

Looking back, I realize that from age eighteen to twenty-four, I was completely stable—apart from one low phase I went through due to a bad break-up. This tells me that bipolar is something that can be easily controlled and managed, and is nothing to fear. If we acknowledge its existence and deal with it in a sensible fashion, instead of denying and ignoring the disorder, we are more likely to avoid future episodes.

My first recovery phase had me seeing therapists while taking regular medication. Since I was in Canada at that time and had my health insurance covered, finding a therapist wasn't difficult. I was also consulting Dr Rajesh Parikh from India at the time. He is also a good friend of my father's. He introduced me to a psychiatrist and professor at Harvard, Dr Gary Sachs, whom I still consult.

Below is the transcript of a Skype conversation I had with Dr Sachs. I was partially manic during this interaction; nonetheless, I am sharing it as I find that the message continues to strike a chord within me and reflects what I was going through then.

Sachs: So, we're talking about trying to build a life that's worth living and the plan for doing that. What would make life worth living for you?

Me: Umm, I feel that life is all about love. Love is life; life is love. That's all there is.

Sachs: How does that connect with not feeling like you can go on, as you were saying just before you decided to record?

Me: Well, I wanted to record [this conversation] because I wanted to keep this forever. I don't ever want to forget this conversation.

Sachs: Well, what I'm actually more concerned with is not whether you're recording or not, but the issue you raised about whether you could go on with life.

Me: Yes ... Life is tiring, but the best part is, if I want to end it, I can end it; if I don't want to end it, I won't end it [and] it's going to end anyway. So, whether I want it or not, one day God will say, 'Okay, you've had enough time in this space, time, universe'... So, it's only a matter of time.

In addition to the medication and getting all the psychiatric help I could, I would attend community dance classes with my friend Cayte. It was here that my interest in Latin dance was born.

These are the only few memories I have of my first episode. I do not want to mention the rest of what I know about the episode as it wouldn't be a first-person account, given that I do not remember those details myself. It would simply be somebody else's observations.

*

In life I seldom had to take on the responsibility of decisions, since I let my parents decide for me. I wanted to pursue acting, but sometime after my first admission to the hospital, due to my diagnosis, I had to face rejection at a high-school musical audition. It left a strong impression on my mind. My father told me that if I could not take rejection well, I would never be able to pursue that line of work. Later, there were times when I would ask him again if I could make it as an actor. Every time he would underline that I could do anything I wanted to and trained myself for. He made me aware about the realities and challenges of being an actor, which proved invaluable as I focused on dance as my calling.

I know my stepfather experienced this too; when he got into the Indian Institute of Technology, his parents stated: 'Your brother has got into the same stream. You should pursue medicine.' Without questioning them, he did what his parents felt he should. Abba held this grudge against his parents for the longest time until he was almost forty-five. Only then did he finally come to realize that no matter what, you cannot hold anyone responsible for your own life's decisions and circumstances.

I was often sad and angry that every moment in my life was defined by whether or not my parents approved, whether society approved and so on. I looked deep within to understand the reasons for this and realized it was because I was constantly seeking attention, approval and validation from those around me, from those I looked up to. It was hard to live up to those expectations. I never understood what those who loved me really meant until recently—all they really wanted was for me to find what I truly loved, what gave me happiness, and for me to give it my best. A saying has been passed down in my family from generations. It goes: *'Chahe gali ka mochi bann, lekin gali ka sabse behtereen mochi bann'* [You can be a cobbler if you so decide, but be the very *best* cobbler on your street].

3

Marriage, Domestic Violence, Divorce

Chaos Opens Its Ugly Mouth

‘Each time a woman stands up for herself without knowing it possibly, without claiming it, she stands up for all women.’

—Maya Angelou

After my marriage, I moved to a city in Europe, far away from my family. Little did I know that I would become a victim of domestic violence during my time there. I was twenty-three when I got married. By twenty-four I had separated from my husband and got divorced at twenty-six.

Arranging Love: A Hasty Decision

While residing with my aunt in the US at the age of twenty-two, I thought that marriage was all fun and play, so I tried to *shop* for a husband online. I created an account on a matrimonial website with the support of my aunt. That's how I found my future husband.

I was in a two-and-a-half-year-long relationship just before this, and the break-up had destroyed me. This ex-boyfriend was a major in the Indian Army. We met in Pune during some Latin dance socials, and we danced the bachata. There was an instant connection. We spent long hours dancing and talking. I used to attend almost every army function he had at the College of Military Engineering (CME) and socialize with the army wives; it almost made me feel like I was married to him.

The break-up resulted in a minor manic episode. I continued seeking out dance to soothe me, and found solace in the Latin rhythms which reached my ears. I held my various dance partners close to me, shutting my eyes and reminiscing the times I had spent with him. It didn't entirely help though, only made things worse.

So, I decided to get married probably to escape. I was young and naive. I viewed marriage as all fun and games. For me it was all a very exciting venture. I wanted a relationship and was eager to build a home with someone. After having seen my parents' divorce as a child, I was convinced that I wouldn't want to have one. It was a kind of goal for me—not to get a divorce. But then again, sometimes we unconsciously tend to follow our parents' footsteps. We grow up seeing a particular pattern of behaviour and while it may or may not appeal to us, we pick it up as children. I could only make these connections later in life, when I re-examined my past. At that time, I wasn't fully aware of why I was choosing marriage at the age of twenty-three.

The first time I met my husband-to-be in person was in Hyderabad, at the Taj hotel. Later we dined at the Taj Falaknuma Palace, which would also be the destination of our wedding. During our initial courtship, we used to have long conversations; he was a scientist and would talk about his interesting research, and since I was an artiste, I used to talk about dance and even perform for him sometimes. He was apparently mesmerized by my dance and my expressions, especially my eyes; I could also take any conversation to a good place. Of course, our courtship was all long distance and digital. The first time we met was the time he proposed to me, and I said yes. He did it respectfully too, asking for my family's permission before asking me.

He was very knowledgeable about bipolar disorder as he studied the brain at work. He would speak as though he was completely prepared to handle anything that came along with my diagnosis, but the truth was far from it. Soon into our marriage, even the littlest things would get on his nerves and he was unable to control his anger towards me.

I have to admit that back then I took great pride in him, especially since he was a self-made man. His father had passed away many years ago, and he wasn't in touch with his mother, who later passed away too. His mother suffered from mental health issues, and I realized that he probably had problems too, but he never spoke of them. I only learnt and deduced one thing from another, especially through what he shared with me of his own early childhood experiences.

Red Flag

I will always regret the way in which I went about my marriage. Particularly in the light of disregarding a certain red flag that manifested before the marriage: my fiancé had slapped me. I was in Hyderabad, it was a scorching summer day, and I was with him in a car, excited and looking forward to some pre-wedding shopping. A few people approached the car and began asking for alms in an aggressive manner which made me anxious. As these people surrounded the car, my husband-to-be left the car to attend a call. On his return I got upset that he wasn't there for me when I needed someone to handle the worsening situation.

I was delivered my first pre-wedding gift: a slap on my left cheek which I can feel even now as I write this. At that time, I decided to not tell my family at large about this incident.

It is uncanny how we are often reluctant to listen to family members once we have decided on a certain course of action. The rebel in us kicks in, often for all the wrong reasons. The more they caution us about something, the more they advise us, the more adamant we become. There is no apparent reason for this, except maybe that we need to learn our own lessons. It was the same with my marriage. I did not know better and went ahead with it despite my family's misgivings.

The marriage was fixed, without a prior engagement ceremony. Had the engagement taken place, it would have been months in advance. If we had done that, I believe we would have never married in the first place. But as they always say, everything happens for a reason.

It is probably the human condition that we gain wisdom only with hindsight. As I reflect on my past today, all these experiences come back to me. But I am extremely grateful that time has allowed me the ability to take these in my stride and begin afresh.

Our honeymoon took place in Srinagar, Kashmir. It was beautiful, but I was yet to discover the fact that he was a smoker; in his profile he was listed as a 'non-smoker'. That was the first blow to really hit me. And then a tattoo on his chest was revealed—an image of a pirate skull. It was hideous. But I was stuck with it and, as I would discover later, with him.

Trouble Picks Up Pace

I must concede that I, too, was very immature at that time. I would have occasional late nights which would sometimes result in me skipping my medicines. Besides, I did not live up to the socially normalized idea of the 'duties of a good wife', like taking care of the home properly. I do not want to get into the possible reasons why a man would choose to raise his hand on his partner. I can only speak for myself. The truth is, while two hands are needed to clap, that can never justify violence; no matter how grave an argument, one must never raise a hand on a fellow human being. There simply is no justification for that.

One night in Dresden, where we were living, something happened that I wasn't proud of. As a consequence, my self-image was shattered because I equated this event, however justifiable, as wrong in principle. The key learning here is to act on a broken relationship, either by ending it in time or by making conscious efforts to fix it. This could be through several methods, including professional counselling, or getting the advice of family and friends to help you navigate the rough times. In retrospect, I wish I had reached out to my family before making what was clearly a hasty decision. I must also say that I do not have any regrets, but yes I experienced guilt. I was in the throes of multiple conflicting emotions. I lost my mind as I knew it, in what doctors would later called a 'mixed episode'. I believe now that my episode was my mind's way of taking a break and making the most of a mental breakdown. I needed to breathe deep and relax before I started to point fingers at myself or my ex-husband.

There were so many thoughts racing in my mind about what had happened, and the small capsule of a marriage that I had experienced at such a tender age. The only person I confided in at the end was my boss, Gabby.

Gabby was also my counsellor and a wonderful support system for me in Germany. A traditional woman, she was against my divorce. She wanted me to work on the marriage. I did try my best. But I think there were too many unresolved issues I was dealing with to be able to give any relationship a chance.

Once, during an interview, when my mother heard me speak such thoughts out loud, the following exchange ensued. It might give an insight into my own thoughts and what a caregiver might go through when dealing with a person with mental health issues.

Shabnam: I think handing you over to a man who wasn't close-by was probably not the right thing to do. I mean, I gave you a lot of ... I thought you could handle it. When I got you married, I thought you were strong enough, you were mature enough, you were well enough to go into this relationship, because you demonstrated a conviction to be married and you so wanted to have a married life and a family that you could call your own. Because somewhere I feel, you felt, '*Oh, my father is remarried, my mother is remarried, they have their own families. I want my own family. I want my own child.*' Am I right?

Me: Yeah, I completely felt that way! Even now, I'm in search of someone whom I can have a family with, have kids with one day. However, there are times I doubt my ability to take up the responsibility. I am not sure I have the strength or the confidence. I don't think it's because of the bipolar, but it could be; but I know that there are many people out there who have bipolar and are happily married. I don't think that's such a grave disability to prevent you from sharing a relationship with someone.

My mother was willing to help share some of the responsibility for what happened. But people don't always do that and end up condemning the person without a full understanding of the situation. That episode has gone a long way towards enabling me to not judge people without being aware of the context in which they act.

*

After the flight from Germany to India, at the end of my marriage, just as I was beginning my separation, I remember having an experience that may help you understand better all that unfolded.

That day after landing I had a long shower in the bathroom of my mother's apartment in Mumbai. I wanted to wash all my memories away. I could feel heightened body sensations. The images of my husband abusing me as I tried to find an escape haunted me. I prayed that this failed marriage wouldn't taint my soul.

I also bit my lips with nervousness. The taste of blood lingered in my mouth. I could feel a sensation in my stomach. I knew what had transpired and I was fully aware of my physical and mental well-being. I consulted a doctor soon after landing in Mumbai. He directed my family towards a rehabilitation centre which was easily accessible, and he was a great support to me in my times of desperate need.

'Keep Trying'

Once back, it didn't take me long to realize that disregarding the red flag at the beginning of our relationship was a mistake. The abuse at the hands of my husband while we were married had escalated pretty early on and was a constant. I had a supportive family, and knew that they would have asked me to come back the moment I wanted to. However, like many other girls my age, I kept trying, hoping the marriage would improve and things would work out.

I finally exited the marriage only after committing infidelity. When this occurred, my ex-husband sent my entire family a 'newsletter' via email, describing in great detail what I had done. He even sent them a voice recording of me talking when I was fully in a manic episode; this was recorded by my sister-in-law. I did not seek police intervention or an organization's support, although in retrospect I wish I had as it may have given me some perspective on my situation.

I know that instances of such silent acceptance of abuse at the hands of the spouse is quite common. Despite all the empowerment women have experienced, there's still a stigma associated with taking your marriage troubles out of closed doors. And this extends to the woman's family too. The situation is only aggravated when you are coping with mental health issues. 'What will people say' is a common refrain. As such, we hold on to the idea that God or the universal power will take care of this for us—through what we call karma. However, that only empowers the perpetrators of domestic violence.

As I 'kept trying', the abuse continued. There were several instances when my ex-husband slapped me. He hated to be woken up from his sleep. He too had mental health issues, as a result of which he had constant nightmares and was a light sleeper. Once, when I woke him up, he flayed both his hands about angrily, slapping me twice. I remember crying uncontrollably. This was just the beginning, a teaser of what was to follow. Little did I know that this would become a pattern of sorts, and unfortunately my brushing it aside also became a recurrent pattern. Another time, on New Year's day, I was watching a TV show, and I hadn't had my medicines; this made him livid. He pulled my laptop away and slapped me on my cheek, insisting that it was time to go to bed and I should immediately take my meds. As you can see, the intention was good, but the method and means of conveying his feelings were purely criminal.

The last time he struck me was twice on my spine—the worst thing he ever did. I will never forget it, and neither will my body. To this day I suffer from pain due to that injury. That day, we had decided to dine outside, but by the time I came back after teaching my Latin dance class it was quite late. I had not eaten anything outside, although I had accompanied the class group to a restaurant. I had explained that I had promised my husband I would join him for dinner.

When I reached home, I found him lying on the couch. He told me he had eaten and said that if I wanted to, I could go out and eat. I simply stated that had he informed sooner, I could have eaten with my friends, but now it was almost eleven in the night. As I was speaking, he rushed towards me from the couch, grabbed me by my hair as I was hunching a little, and with his elbow struck me on my back, exactly on my spinal cord, twice.

That day, I ran away from home to spend the night at a common friend, Fatima's place. She and her husband were kind enough to keep me. I wish I had given up and exited the relationship that day itself. I went back the next morning, but my feelings for him had died.

Bitter Memories

Just before leaving Germany, another incident occurred. I had confided in my distant relative, whom I considered a sister-in-law, about the fact that I had been disloyal to my husband. By this point of time, I was already in my manic phase. Little did I know that my voice would be recorded on a phone. This voice recording was then sent to my husband. I had said some very terrible and mean things. I didn't know it would backfire so badly. My mother, too, was sent this recording later.

I say this not with the intention of washing my dirty linen in public: I simply want to urge people to be sensitive and aware that someone who is acting in a certain way may perhaps be doing so because they are not mentally stable. It can be very hard to not take someone seriously sometimes, but one must learn to differentiate between a person's illness and their personality. I have also lost many friendships due to the harsh words I have said during manic moments. Words are like daggers, and once they are uttered, they cannot be taken back.

This doesn't mean one can blame all of one's actions and words on one's disorder and use it as an excuse for bad behaviour all the time. But one should try to see the larger picture and cultivate a level of sensitivity and awareness.

Reflections on Domestic Violence

For most people, things like rape, domestic violence, death and tragedies exist only when they happen to them or someone they know. We live in a bubble and think that these things won't happen to us. This I know from personal experience. Having lived for almost a year in an abusive marriage, I know that we are invariably unprepared for it, and we lose the ability to respond to something like this when it happens.

In retrospect, I constantly wonder why I took it all for a whole year. I often complained to my doctor in Dresden about my husband hitting and abusing me. In response, my doctor would always advise me to exit the relationship, especially since I have bipolar disorder. 'If you did not have this condition, I wouldn't necessarily insist that you exit from this relationship,' he said. I did not take this advice, although I now know that I should have.

At the time, my mother was admitted to a hospital for an operation and I even wanted to return to India for that reason. My father tried to protect me from being exposed to my mother's illness, but didn't know that I was suffering in my marriage in Europe. In fact, even when he visited me in Germany, I never mentioned the abuse to him.

After all this time, I know that abuse is something that can drive women to do things they are later not proud of, things they ordinarily wouldn't do. Abuse not only bruises the body, it bruises the mind and soul of a human being. It's a very deep cut and it takes time to heal.

It is important for women to take a stand as individuals against abuse of any kind. The moment we accept being in an abusive relationship, it not only persists but somewhere inside us the behaviour becomes acceptable. If we do not take a stand and stop it the moment it occurs, chances are that the abuse will continue and become fatal. Many a times, especially if we do not get support from our families, we feel there is absolutely no way out.

I urge everyone going through domestic violence, and even friends and family members who know of anyone in an abusive relationship, to tackle it before it gets too late. Today, many countries, including India, have helpline numbers and places where one can reach out for support.

One can also get referrals in the form of counsellors or support groups.

I hope that things change more rapidly, especially in rural India. If we as a society take a stand against domestic violence, change wouldn't just be a dream, it could well become a reality.

Another thing our Indian society added to the long list of unwarranted taboos is divorce. I know this is changing, but if somebody is divorced, it is still usually much harder for them to be accepted or have a fresh beginning in life. One of the biggest problems of our society is that they would rather have people live in a defunct marriage than get a divorce and live on their own terms. Many a times women are not financially independent, which also restricts their options. This of course is not an attack on men. I know of a friend whose ex-wife used to raise her hand on him. This happens less often perhaps, but we all have to be mindful that things such as these do occur and we must ensure that they are also not accepted.

If our society comes to terms with the fact that something can go wrong in a marriage and accepts that there is nothing wrong with separation and divorce, I think we would be in a much better place. Of course, when there are children, it gets even more complicated, as it did in my parents' case, but that's no reason to put up with violence, abuse, or even persistent unhappiness.

The Questionable Terms of Marriage and Separation

When I separated from my ex-husband, he demanded that I return all the jewellery he had given me at the time of our marriage. This made me feel like a commodity or like a failed investment.

When my beloved late uncle and I discussed the matter, he explained to me the Hindu concept of *streedhan*. He said that it referred to the right of a woman over the wealth given to her in marriage; I didn't owe this man anything. My aunt, however, had a somewhat different opinion. She stated that since my marriage lasted legally for less than a year and I separated in merely eleven months, I had no right over what he had given me.

All of these experiences prompted me to ask: What defines a 'legitimate' marriage? Isn't any marriage, however short or long in duration, a valid union? If religious rituals brought us together and legal documents made it valid for society, what then is the definition of divorce? Isn't divorce a legal document produced by our society? Are there ritualistic or religious provisions to provide for divorce?

In any case, I finally did not accept an alimony from my ex-husband, going by the simple principle that I did not want to be financially dependent on any man, and least of all my ex-husband who had abused me emotionally and physically. My father helped me arrive at this decision, which I respect entirely. I do not have any regrets about it even now.

4

A New Dawn

Fresh Beginnings

Everything happens for a reason and it is all ultimately for the best, we are told. It took me two years to recover from the trauma of domestic violence I experienced in Germany. But my marriage not only taught me valuable lessons, it transformed me entirely and made me a more responsible adult, opening up a whole new world for me.

I had learnt to survive in a faraway town on my own, away from my family. I had learnt to run a home—from cooking and cleaning to inviting friends home and organizing social gatherings. I learned the responsibilities that come with having two or three jobs and earning for a household. From teaching Latin dance in a middle school to teaching Kathak privately, I had a range of activities that would keep me occupied. I had the opportunity to interact with new people and the chance to explore new places. I even performed Kathak in many places—from a café filled with immigrants to a church full of German Christians. I formed innumerable bonds with dancers, my employer, and of course my ex-husband's friends, including those from the South Asian community in Dresden. Exploring the city through the public transport system was yet another chance at freedom and responsibility that I thoroughly enjoyed.

Despite all the progress you have made in life, when you are rejected by someone because you have 'lost your mind', society sort of dictates that you must feel pathetic and sorry for yourself. So, for society's sake I sulked and wallowed in my misery and was single for almost a year. The fear of never ever being with someone would gnaw at me little by little every day. I would take out my frustration by binge eating and my weight increased by 30 kilograms. When I couldn't even look at myself any more, the fear of never having someone in my life materialized again and so I continued to stay single.

But this had its own advantages. I began to have ample time to study for my Early Childhood Education Programme and would devote long hours to learning Kathak. My relationship with my family members improved as I wasn't using up all my precious hours talking to strangers any more. I realized this had to take place for me to truly understand the importance of my family; they never reject me, whatever state I might be in, and they accepted me for whoever I eventually turned out to be.

Dalhousie Public School

While all this growth was great, the fact remained that my marriage had been extremely traumatic. My experience at the Dalhousie Public School, a boarding school, helped me overcome the trauma resulting from the nightmarish experience.

When I was returning from Germany, I was mid-episodic on the flight. So, I had to be admitted to a rehab hospital on arrival. I stayed in three different rehabs for a period spanning from six to nine months, and it was primarily my experience at Dalhousie Public School and the pure beings that inhabited it that actually healed me. Their kindness and love have proven to be a catalyst in my well-being.

I joined Dalhousie Public School in 2016 as a pre-primary teacher, hostel in-charge and dance teacher. The whole idea of sending me there after my divorce was that I would be close to family while working, as I was still recovering from my marriage. The director and chairman of the school, Dr Guru Dhillon, is my father's dear friend. He had met him when he was shooting the film *1942: A Love Story* at the same school. Besides, as a child I had visited Dalhousie with my mother.

My experience at DPS introduced me to the pleasures of simple uncluttered living. Both teachers and children found joy in long walks, examining their surroundings, being one with nature. It was not always easy for some of the teachers as they had to live for long durations without their respective families or partners. For those who hadn't settled down yet it wasn't an ideal place to find a match due to limited options. Thinking back, perhaps this is what made me leave too. However, there are times that I regret the decision because the happiest moments of my life have been in Dalhousie. Especially when I was in charge of teaching the high-school girls Kathak. I also taught preschool and kindergarten children dance movements, art and games. I thoroughly enjoyed engaging with young minds and found the ambience to apply my faith in using arts as a means of education.

During this phase of my life, I interacted with many people and made many new friends. Despite living in a place with little adult human interaction, I became very good friends with my senior supervisor, Rashmi Thakur. She was a sister, mother, counsellor and friend, all rolled into one.

The job gave me the opportunity to thrive at something I loved: working with young children. I thoroughly enjoy spending time with children. Seeing them smiling and happy while also imparting a good education made me feel accomplished. I had faith in using the arts as a means of education. In doing so, I immersed young minds in dance, yoga, art and learning in natural environments. I believe that a job is not only about making a steady income but also a means of making a positive difference in your community. And this one allowed me to do just that. It also helped me discover my emerging passion for early childhood education.

My experience with the children at the school taught me that they are the purest beings on the face of the planet. Very rarely do we come across adults who have retained the childlike quality of pure love and giving. For instance, unlike many adults, children are quick to notice changes in your moods or appearance.

I know this because whenever I have a rough day, I do not wear my kajal (kohl) and lipstick, and they would invariably be the first ones to notice. On one such day, one of my students came up to me and pointed out the absence of lipstick, while remarking that I look so pretty with it on. She also suggested that I choose shoes like the ones her mother wore and was trying to describe them through gestures as she did not seem to know the word 'heels'. Children are most generous in giving compliments, because they do not have a big ego.

Unfortunately, we often look forward to children growing up soon, and today, children themselves want to mature even faster than is required of them. It doesn't occur to us that perhaps the best qualities of a human being are given to us at birth and we may in fact be unconsciously ridding ourselves of all these qualities and creating an environment of hate and negativity as we grow older.

At school I had very few hours of loneliness; I was at peace spending time with my schoolchildren or surrounded by natural beauty. At times, during prep duty in school, I would just stare out at a tree and observe a bird. How often in our busy lives do we get time to do this? I can assure you there is immense satisfaction in observing nature. The more we indulge in acts like this, the more we realize just how beautiful life really is.

People's happiness quotient is crucial and largely determined by their degree of materialism. An obsession with money and objects, as opposed to forming special bonds with friends and family, leads us away from happiness. A Harvard study has shown that the happiest people are the ones with the most successful human connections. It is crucial that we as humans try and be as social as possible. I read somewhere that being alone and being lonely are two very different things, and at DPS I was seldom lonely.

I faced judgement at times for being divorced, albeit very rarely. However, I must state that there were several single mothers and teachers in the school, and I wasn't the only one. This phenomenon is experienced in most parts of the country, and a particular place or set of people cannot be blamed for this mindset.

Labels, societal norms and expectations can only impact us negatively if we allow our environment to dictate the way we view ourselves. For example, in my case, if I were to identify with all the stigma that is associated with my disorder, and apply it to myself, not only would I be unable to function in society, it would be extremely painful to be constantly rejected.

Self-love and acceptance are for me of utmost importance today. I realize when the world is against you, the only person really rooting for you is yourself; and when the world is with you, the only person you have with you, again, is yourself! So, in a way, it would mean that the best thing to happen to you would be for you to fall deeply in love with yourself, so that each action of yours protects your interests.

Whether we believe it or not, we come and go alone, so we have to accept ourselves, and if we have problems with the way we function, we have to make a conscious effort to turn things around. The very fact that we try to make things better is what makes life worth it. Instead of not making any efforts at all, and waiting for a miracle, we have to be the catalyst for miracles to manifest. Because miracles do not just happen, we must make them happen.

I realize that self-love is also important because no matter how many doctors and therapists one sees (in my case for bipolar disorder), at the end of the day, the key to making things right is in our hands. Only *I* can change my physical and mental health through exercise and by taking my medications on time. No one else will do it for me. All we have is ourselves, so we might as well make ourselves the strongest pillar in our own lives.

Return to Canada

I returned to Canada in 2018 after I left Dalhousie Public School. I will forever cherish the memories and experiences at Dalhousie Public School. They gave me the confidence in pursuing my interests in child education. However, at that point all of us felt that moving to Canada would be best for my mental and physical well-being.

One of the main reasons for this was that they knew Canada to be a land where not only are people's diverse cultural backgrounds respected, but also a place that is inclusive for differently-abled persons. In hindsight, being in Canada helped me much more than I thought it would at the time because a divorced woman is excluded in many sections of Indian society. Besides, most people are made to believe that it is a reason to be ashamed of themselves and feel that they are less than others. I have experienced this myself in the quest for relationships I sought at the time.

For instance, I have faced rejection by the family of my boyfriends due to my divorced status and/or especially because of my mental health. This reality was a major catalyst in me choosing to move to Toronto, Canada, as I was aware that the overall acceptance and talk surrounding mental health was not only not a taboo but was openly encouraged. After moving to Canada, I was pleasantly surprised to enter a world where being bipolar did not render me an outcast from society. In fact, in many ways I have felt like an outcast in big Indian gatherings, and as I grew older I preferred not to attend many social events in India. I could never get over the feeling that I was being judged and people were looking at me, talking about me, or were conscious in my presence.

I always knew that I would miss Dalhousie Public School—the natural surroundings, the children, Mrs Annu Dhillon and Dr Guru Dhillon, who provided me with the support and counselling I desperately needed, as well as my mentor and dear friend Rashmi Ma'am.

*

'Hyper but functional.' This sentence may merely consist of three words, but it aptly defines my state during my last episode in December of 2019. These are the words of Dr Gary Sachs, whom I've been consulting for over a decade now.

Dr Sachs has been an incredible support as a caregiver and counsellor. His entire approach is the collaborative care system framework within which the patient identifies three or more central figures in their lives who can provide care, comfort and, most importantly, advice in the time of crisis.

In this case it was my mother, my father and my late uncle Vir Papa. I used these supports constantly to help me in all areas to tide over my hurdles.

Another aspect of my relationship with Dr Sachs is the advice he provides me with for medications. Advising me on when it is the right time to take a blood test, reviewing the blood tests for me, adjusting medications, etc. Life advice, however, is the favourite aspect of my interactions with him. Whenever I have an appointment with him there is almost always something to learn and apply in my own life from it!

Before I set off on my most recent trip to India, Dr Sachs advised me not to go. He was right to caution me about my decision, and he also did tell me that there were many things that I would learn from my mistakes—and that it would be a great learning experience. Looking back, I think: Which experience in life is not a learning experience? We do not always apply the learnings we have acquired from our past experiences; but the learning itself is always there, to be absorbed and internalized.

For me, this particular trip to India was indeed an eye-opening experience. During this journey I learnt what two jet lags experienced over a period of two weeks can do to me, or to anyone coping with bipolar for that matter. I have now become an 'aware' bipolar as a result of it, which is to say that I am so conscious of my symptoms and illness that when they manifest, I can tell the exact size of the waves of the predicted tsunami that will swallow me. Being able to do this, unfortunately, is not enough. To go along with this metaphor a bit longer, one may say: I need to know surfing. The first step in learning to surf is to eradicate the fear of the unknown. This, I believe, is the hardest part of dealing with bipolar. For me, each episode has been so unique in its essence that it is hard to predict what may occur when I am episodic.

However, luckily I know one thing for certain: that once you find your own 'cure', by which I mean understanding your own set of coping mechanisms that work for you, the unknown is easier to deal with.

For me, during this episode, the unknown was difficulty sleeping—not necessarily sleepless nights by definition, for I would sleep for six to seven hours each day, which is more than sufficient for an active mind and body. However, my father's words kept reverberating in my ears: 'If only she understands how important sleep is, she will be fine.' My question here to him was this: 'Father, if I close my eyes, and only see colours in all forms and shapes—blue, red, green—moving in different patterns, changing rhythms, and then I open my eyes to pitch darkness but see the exact same thing, what should I do?'

The answer to this question presented itself to me in December 2019 in Pune, where I was residing at the time with my Kathak guru, Pta Maneesha Sathe, following the guru–shishya parampara. When I had a nightmare one night, I ran to my guru's room with full faith because I knew that, no matter what, her presence would rescue me. And a rescue is exactly what unfolded. She gave me few spiritual phrases to recite in my mind before sleeping. It worked its magic. Way better than counting sheep!

5

The Many Meanings of Dance

Therapy, Coping Mechanism, Life

My parents have always stood by me and helped me come to terms with their divorce and its impact on me. I have a transcript of an interview with my mother which was recorded as part of her MFA thesis research on mental health. In it, the ideas I had shared with my mother capture not just the ways in which she helped me, but also how dance enabled me to deal with my parents' divorce and the many binaries that had come to define my life. At the time, I was choreographing a dance piece on different kinds of love, and this is what I said:

> Since I have learnt so many forms, I always thought that I had to choose between one or the other and [...] I think because I put myself under this pressure of having to choose between one or the other, [and] because I have always presented myself with that dilemma [...] it's either black or white. [...] So even in my life, talking about choices between India and Canada, I had to go to Canada because my mother had my sole custody, but it continued being a 'choice' that I would think about; India, or Canada? Mom, or dad? ... and I think I also, in a weird way, because of my diagnosis, [as it is implicit] in its very

> definition, I had to choose between – Am I high or am I low? But you know what? Maybe I am neither. It doesn't have to be just one. And when I dance, I realize that I can express myself in a variety of ways. I dance to honour my Kathak guru, Odissi guru, classical dance [guru or] Latin ballroom teacher. I just feel that art is something that you can't quantify and that you can't put rules to, and definitely to some extent you need to know the rules to break them, but sometimes I feel that the very fear of wanting to break the rules puts you in a constraint and compartmentalizes you and this is simply my attempt to merge and bring together all that defines one's movement through space.

*

Dance therapy consists of more than what the words denote. Dance is not simply movement through space but a way of life. Getting up early in the morning, having a bath, doing the morning prayers or talking to yourself or the higher power or universe, and with a cleansed mind and body making your way to your guru's home and offering yourself in learning the artform while also being a strong support to your guru. Once you become a dancer and make a conscious decision to devote yourself to dance, the therapeutic nature of dance will automatically follow. Dance is not simply the dancer's relationship with the artform, but with her guru, with her guru's disciples, and eventually her audience too. Dance as therapy or coping mechanism helps one negotiate the experiences one goes through in their life, and gives the opportunity to reflect on it artistically.

While I was married, I would focus on my dance, no matter whatever abuse would take place at home, and honestly, it was liberating because I would dance to whatever I wanted to and expressed my creativity in any form of my choice, including fusion pieces with other dancers from around the globe. I also took the opportunity to attend the International Tango Dance Congress with my dance partner, Kalyan Shencottah, who came to Dresden to meet me. I think this was part of a longer pattern where from a young age dance was an escape.

After my divorce, I stopped dancing for over two years. The divorce impacted me so badly that I gave up the one activity I cherished most. In my trauma and confusion, I did not know who to reach out to. As I have mentioned, I married against the advice of my family. So, I was reluctant to go back to them with my woes. However, in my fragile state I was also unable to take a decision on my own. And like it often happens in cases of depression, you withdraw from the very things you love.

Looking back, I know that the effects of mania in general include an increased surge of creativity. I channelized this into painting, dancing and practising yoga. The energy

I had inside me had to be utilized in a positive way, lest it resulted in negative outcomes. My practice of yoga included Suryanamaskara, cat and camel poses, Parvatasana, and other poses to improve flexibility, posture and strength.

This tendency to pursue creative and spiritual activities is quite common among people with bipolar going through an episode. During such an episode, the person may be drawn to and associate themselves with a higher power, whichever one it may be.

I too used to indulge in these activities when I was hospitalized. Most recently in 2019, where they had provided us with a gym and yoga room. The room overlooked a waterbody, and it was one of the most beautiful sights, especially at sunrise when I would be wide awake due to lack of sleep. Most of my work in general is closely linked with spirituality.

*

During all my years with dance, I had never imagined that there would be a time when I would stop. I did, right after my marriage, which left me shattered. It was only at Dalhousie Public School that I eventually got back to dancing and teaching young children the artform.

Now I know that I may have left dance for a while, but my dance never left me, even if I may not have truly mastered it. It stayed and sustained me. I don't see it as a means to an end, or simply a hobby. I pursue it because it fosters bliss within me. Even when I was hospitalized, my dance never left my side. On my worst days, I would write my Kathak bols, which always helped to calm my mind. For all of this, I am grateful.

I do practise dance today, but it is not a profession. I still enjoy every second while I learn Kathak. I am forever grateful to my guru Pta Maneesha Sathe for being there for me, even when I wasn't truly there for her as a committed student. I now learn from Prajakta Dravid who has given my dance skills a new lease of life.

*

Dance is therapy. We all know this, but I have lived it. Being told something and experiencing the same thing are two entirely different things. Dance is like meditation, where the dancer is free of all worldly thoughts and transcends this universe. The world of a dancer doesn't have any notion of abnormality or normality in it. Everything is pure and sacred, much like the white drapes of Goddess Saraswati. It is this world that I want to live in, devoid of any judgement or labels. The chaos of our thoughts can be silenced through dance, making it possible to soak in the beauty of the world's creation by achieving stillness.

6

Hello, Rejection

A Return to the Dating Scene

Often we come up with the idea of a 'perfect' model of a human being in our minds and begin to imagine our partner to be this person. Without truly examining our partner's true nature, we believe that such a person is guaranteed to provide us all the joy in the world. Is it important to have a list of reasons in order to love someone? Isn't love the only thing in the world which has no reason and needs no purpose to justify its existence?

I have been rejected due to my bipolar several times. I often wonder what percentage of my entire personality is dictated by this illness. It was definitely crushing when a partner or a friend left me mid-episode. It was not easy to return to normalcy and find that the person I considered my partner had abandoned me for another woman while I was in hospital. I didn't receive proper closure in such cases, since I was unable to recall many conversations that I had during my episode. I feel it is absolutely essential to explain to your partner what it is you have and what it might mean for them.

I once met a man in Pathankot, Punjab, using a dating app. It isn't the best way to look for a partner but I wasn't complaining. Having lived in a hill station with little or no contact with any man, I was left with no other option but to search for a partner online.

When I finally arrived at the location we had decided on, I discovered that it was a small, three-storeyed structure, and although it was a mall, it looked more like a tiny dilapidated building within a residential block. When I made my way inside, I couldn't find him. After a while I realized I was waiting at the wrong mall, and he on the other hand had thought that I had taken one good look at him and run away!

I was considering getting into a relationship more than three years after my divorce. I still recall decking myself with a red kurti and silver jhumkis and wearing matching lipstick to go and meet this complete stranger. The first test was getting into an unknown man's vehicle. This went off smoothly. I didn't wind up dead. I passed the test of trust between a couple because I did not question his character or intentions by refusing to get into his car on our very first meeting. It was an exciting adventure for me. Two of my colleagues at DPS accompanied me as 'bodyguards' on this four-hour car journey through a mountainous terrain to a remote city in Punjab.

One thing I realize looking back years later is that it took guts and strength to get back in the so-called 'dating game'. I called him daily for the first week, only to learn that this isn't how the dice is rolled. I was much too eager and ecstatic to have a man in my life once again, one who wouldn't yell at me and beat me up. However, after he explained to me that he was simply busy with work, I took the hint and stopped displaying my eagerness to be loved.

We dated on and off for a period of two years and eventually, even if unofficially, exchanged rings. He met my parents, but I did not get the opportunity to meet his family. Finally, he left me for someone else while I was in the hospital due to an episode.

While dating, sometimes you get insecure and your self-esteem hits rock bottom. This is, of course, one end of the spectrum. The other is that you emerge with greater confidence from within and may find yourself ready to shake the world up.

In Indian society, a great deal of importance is placed upon a woman getting married and having a family of her own. Unfortunately, as a twenty-five-year-old young woman with many peers doing the same, I let this idea of finding the perfect husband and having a married life get to my head to such an extent that I left my job at Dalhousie Public School and moved to Mumbai in search of a partner.

Rejection: Relationships and Mental Health

For the first time in my life at the age of twenty-five, my partner's parents rejected me because of my bipolar disorder. What is the real reason behind conservative older generations refusing to accept someone who is on medications for bipolarity? Is it the fear of the unknown? Some say marriages are made in heaven. My experience has impressed upon me that it is merely a business transaction—something similar to buying a product in the market, especially one with a lifetime warranty. In reality, can we get a lifetime guarantee on relationships? In some cases, a person has all the supposed desirable qualities—a good education and a steady income. We get blinded by these qualities, but in the end, they cease to matter if the person is not a compassionate and honest human being at heart. Many a times, people's vices are disguised in their qualifications and net worth. Is money so important that we fail to see the real human qualities in a person? It would be a different world if we married for love instead of a list of requirements that appear to make a partner worthy of marriage.

At times, the biggest challenge one faces under these mental conditions is the inability to take an informed decision and having to depend on others. That often creates a situation where you are left conflicted. I wanted to return to Mumbai after my work in Dalhousie but decided against it, given that it would mean that I would be leaving behind the man I was dating at that point in my life. But lo and behold, a few weeks later, as I stayed back at the school to teach, the man's parents rejected me due to my mental health.

I clearly remember two encounters I had with his mother. The first evening, we spent almost five hours together; we conversed, laughed, shared food (I even cooked a meal for everyone—an act that would presumably have satisfied any typical Indian mother-in-law). Soon after, the second meeting followed; this was a dark, intense encounter. I entered their one-bedroom apartment which was on the top floor in a deserted area. As soon as I entered, I saw the lifeless, ghostly expression of his mother staring at me. I sat down nervously. Judging by how my attempts at striking up a conversation were met, I couldn't shake the feeling that she was not only exuding hate towards me, but seemed petrified of me. At that moment I became aware that she had been informed about my mental health condition. It was tragic and, at the same time, amusing. I told myself that I do not need to prove to anyone in this world that I am 'sane' or 'normal'. Besides, to spend an entire life with a woman who was convinced that I was an alien, didn't seem worth my time.

There will be a few who accept you, and even when most don't, the silver lining is that the person who accepts you, accepts all of you and for who you really are, makes it all worth it. This is truly an act that only an inclusive, non-judgemental and evolved person can do. Patience and acceptance are empowering qualities, and might be enough in a partner, a friend, or a loved one. However, the bottom line is that an individual, to the best degree possible, must accept and love their own condition and truly own it. If my illness was a person, I would want to hug it and love it. At the end of the day, it is a part of me, not the whole of me, and not necessarily an ugly one. It should, according to me, be embraced and even flaunted.

I do know of one such person who truly accepted each aspect of their partner's personality, illness included: my nani or maternal grandmother. My grandfather, the famous film-maker S. Sukhdev, struggled with undiagnosed mental health issues. He was an alcoholic who sometimes in his drunken state was abusive. Although he would act this way at times, my grandma stood by his side. She never let him feel he had an illness or that something was amiss, although his behaviour would say otherwise. She was an emotional pillar to him, and he would confide in her his deepest thoughts and feelings. His actions were driven partly by the fact that he loved my grandma to bits and partly by his mental condition, which he had no control over. Looking back, there is no doubt how unfair the marriage was to my grandmother. It also demonstrates the societal conditions at the time which made it impossible for a woman to walk out of an abusive relationship. He passed away after a third heart attack at the age of forty-six, leaving behind several documentaries that continue to uphold his legacy on celluloid. My grandma was widowed young, but she never remarried, although she received several proposals.

She chose to continue to live with a man who abused her, and it will always remain a dilemma: How far should one be willing to go to support a person who has a mental health condition? Once my mother questioned my grandmother about her reasons for not leaving her husband. She responded, 'When you love someone enough, these things cease to matter.' In my view, my grandma should have taken help from family members or some counsellors to help my grandfather.

However, her own level of suffering was too much, and she tried her best to do what she could. And these were not times when these issues were discussed openly or addressed medically, and in some instances even now this is the case.

Ultimately, it is we who have to accept ourselves and our disorder in the first place, for that would eventually empower us the most. The more we accept the disorder, as a mere condition that needs constant care and concern, the more others will find it easier to accept us. I know that accepting ourselves is easier said than done. However, we must constantly work towards not undermining ourselves, especially on account of having a mental health diagnosis.

After having been through multiple heartbreaks, it is now clear to me that the only way to really sustain a secure bond and relationship is to have an extremely strong foundation. The best way to approach this is to form a friendship with someone first. Sometimes it remains a friendship, and sometimes it may transform into love. Of course, in some cases we know right away that we may never view a person as a partner, but sometimes life has the most beautiful surprises in store for us. The best thing to do is to let go and let the universe surprise us. It is important to have faith in the plan the universe has for us; it will save us the stress, anger and resentment towards the way events unfold in our lives.

With my mom, 1991, photo taken by my father

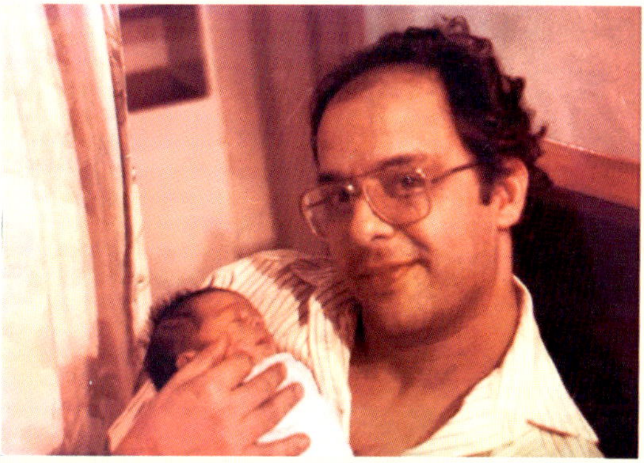

As a new-born with my proud father – his first experience of fatherhood

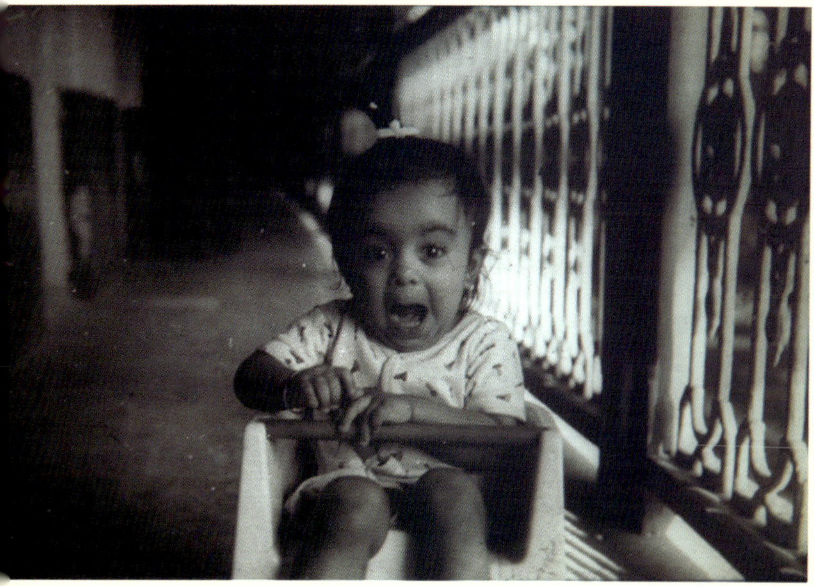

s a baby at FTII, Pune (Film and Television Institute of India), clicked by my mother r a film project

With mom

With my uncle
Vir Papa – I w
always smiling
and happy wi
him, he was li
a father to me

With Dad and
Vir Papa

With my sister Zuni as a baby on my lap and my brother Agni as a toddler

At the Sahyadri residential school with Anjana Akka and my friends

This picture was taken with my beloved Ma (Dadi) on her first trip back to Kashmir, since the family relocated, for the shooting of my dad's movie *Mission Kashmir*

On Dal Lake, Srinagar, in traditional attire on a family trip

With Nani, my mother's mother – I spent most of my childhood with her while my mother was studying

With Nani, after my first-year Kathak exam at Bharathi Vidyapeeth University under the guidance of Guru Pta Maneesha Sathe

With my husband, Biswarup Das: Love is indeed like a butterfly that comes and sits on your shoulder when you least expect it

With Mom and my brother Ishan

My first Kathak performance at Tilak Smarak Mandir, Pune

With Anu-mummy, Dad, and Agni

With my pet beagle, Dobby – pet therapy is the best!

With my brothers, Ishan and Agni

Family: with Abba, Mom and Ishan

Peacock

Rainforest

Om

Firepots in the wild

7

Negotiating Family

The Good, the Bad, and the Ugly

It is extremely strenuous, stressful and traumatic for the caregivers of a patient (especially in my case) to pretend that all is well and that complete recovery is possible after a string of episodes. In my case, I forget my episodes and everything that takes place during that time. It is as if my brain wipes out the negativity entirely to help me heal and look forward instead of feeling embarrassed and stressed about past events that may not even have taken place had I been well at the time. But my caregivers do not have this advantage.

This is something that I experienced with my passion for Latin dance. What made it worse for me was that my engagement with Latin dance often came at the expense of my mental and physical well-being. My caregivers realized its insidious effects which I was oblivious to. Given a couple of experiences I had, whenever I wanted to pursue anything remotely related to Latin dance, I would ask myself repeatedly whether dancing with several male dancers affected me in any manner. A more rational mind would have probably realized that my experiences had nothing to do with Latin dance per se but my volatile state of mind. Latin dance also meant late evenings going into the night. Late nights meant aggravation of my bipolar disorder.

For this reason, whenever I wanted to pursue anything remotely related to Latin dance, my family would get very concerned. As if breaking up of relationships wasn't enough, it seemed that the bipolar issue was causing my break up with Latin dance too.

I had experienced a bipolar episode while doing Latin dance in Pune. Whenever I would mention returning to Latin dance, unpleasant scenes would unfold. During one such episode, I created an audio file for my mother, the text of which captures my state of mind at the time:

> Wednesday, 29 May 2018
>
> When I am sick, I get drawn to Latin dance and that leads to sleeping late and that makes me sicker. I can't do performances, because it is too stressful. So, anything that I really want to do, I'm not able to do. I don't know what to do, Mom, I'm really lost.
>
> Everything is a mess. People think that I have been saying strange things and that I am sick. I do not know how to handle things as they stand. I keep hearing people say, 'Your meds need to be adjusted.' I consulted two counsellors yesterday and both think I am fine. So, I want to ask these people who think I am sick if they are qualified to tell me

whether I am fine or not. Maybe I am not feeling right these days...

Breaking the Ice

I grew up constantly bottling up my thoughts and feelings towards my father and his entire side of the family. I would keep everything inside and not share my feelings. I now realize that the more we talk about the issues we have, the better it is for any relationship. The relationships between parents and children are often prickly. In India we tend to brush any unpleasantness under the carpet of tradition. I have tried to steer clear of this and be honest in my approach.There are various dynamics to human relationships that we often close our minds to. This is something we often fail to realize. This understanding also helped bring a sea change in my relationship with my father. Our relationship is in a much happier place now because of the attempts to foster better communication. For instance, I can't remember the last time a day went by when we didn't speak over a call or a video call. The truth is that if you do not blow off steam where it is required, it will manifest elsewhere. We have to realize that human relationships are more resilient than we give them credit for. It is an uncomfortable process; it may often feel like walking on eggshells, but once you break them, at least the fear of breaking them is eliminated.

The Kindness of Strangers and Others Not So Kind

When I'd finally decided to end my marriage and leave Dresden, I felt intense fear. To overcome it, I made my way back home. I knew I had reached a point of no return, and I needed family around me. With a strong survival instinct, I packed only a suitcase. I filled it with my dance shoes, ghungroos and jewellery which included my chuda (set of bangles a newly-wed Punjabi bride wears). I knew I had to travel light and take only the important things with me because I was in a delicate state. The priority was to reach home safely. I had a train ride to another city in Germany, from where I would have two connecting flights to Mumbai.

On the flight I had a few miraculous experiences. An elderly lady was sitting next to me. Not only did I discover that she was a follower of the Radha Soami sect, like my mother and nani, she also happened to be flying from Edmonton, Alberta, which is where I had lived for six years from the age of twelve. She handed me a laminated photo of her Guru which I kept with me when I was in rehab. Of course after a certain point she requested that her seat be changed because I was talking far too much!

On the same flight, I saw the person sitting next to me watching a movie. I had a glimpse of a few frames which showed my father carrying a small baby in his arms. I even took a picture of the screen so that my family would believe me. Even I needed to convince myself that I was not hallucinating. After seeing the photograph my mother confirmed that it was indeed my father's image on celluloid that I had witnessed at night alone on a flight. What a miracle, as if the universe was speaking to me!

In a manic episode, one often starts blabbering constantly and speaking rapidly. I remember I had to lock myself in the airplane bathroom for minutes at a stretch because I would talk to myself. I was filled with a magnitude of thoughts which would come all too fast for me to process. I confided in a female flight attendant and requested her, 'Can you please remove the mirror because I can see myself and it is bothering me. I want to be alone.' You will not believe it if I told you what happened next: She entered the bathroom cubicle and removed the mirror so I could be with myself in a closed room. It was a long flight. A few hours later, I asked the same favour from a somewhat elderly male flight attendant. The response was hilarious! He said something like 'what, are you crazy!', shouted at me and completely freaked out. Perhaps he was the one who needed more help than I did.

When I landed in India, in the middle of my mixed episode, I was treated with a lot of care. The people at the airport were compassionate. They knew I was ill and something was wrong. I remember a policeman asking my mother if he could help at all in any way. My mother said it was all okay and took me home.

I was soon taken to the hospital. I was aware of what I was going through, all my bodily and mental sensations, and still had no control over them. It was an extremely scary feeling. Some patients have lesser awareness but I have always been very aware of my feelings and emotions. Each time I fell sick I knew I was going through an episode and something was amiss, but there was nothing I could do about it.

Another clear memory I have in the hospital is of pain. I was reminded of my ex-husband. So I stood in front of the mirror and slapped myself. I recalled Eckhart Tolle's concept of pain-body as articulated in *The Power of Now*. My pain-body was immediately awakened when I did that. I would slap myself and then cry and remember him. It was sick, but this pain-body is also what eventually led me to arrive at the decision of filing for divorce. That is when I knew it was over. I cried for the last time and wiped my tears.

My trauma was severe. The gentleman who ran the medical facility resembled my ex. The moment I saw him I yelled, 'Get him away from me.' I remember this clearly. The moment I could face him without reacting I knew I was well. I remember while leaving the hospital, I told him, 'Hope to see you again and thank you so much.' He replied, 'I hope I never have to see you here again.' I smiled because I understood.

After I was discharged from the hospital, one of the doctors who was an intern at the facility at the time contacted me on Facebook. I accepted the invitation thinking he had been my counsellor and I saw nothing wrong in the friendship. However, later, he went on to tell me accounts of how in my manic state I had expressed my attraction towards him. Hearing this I didn't know how to react because at that time I was still recovering. I look back on the episode as an unforgivable breach of the sanctity of the relationship between a doctor and a patient. He not only took advantage of my sick condition at that time but reminded me of a time of which I had no memory as I was not in the right mental state. I am not sharing this to point fingers at the medical fraternity. But to highlight the fact that the doctor-patient relationship is sacrosanct and should be treated with respect and never violated.

Unfortunately, our society is unable to stand up for the rights of women, especially when the woman has committed acts considered 'wrong' by society. This leaves women vulnerable at all times. More so if they are dealing with mental health issues. I was in a loveless marriage and simply did not know how to handle the situation. I, too, was clueless about what I was experiencing. I should have stepped back and made a conscious decision to move back to India, but I didn't—as it often happens in cases of abuse.

Sexual Abuse of People Dealing with MHIs

I was once given a ride to my residence by a colleague. On the way, he got overly personal, using uncalled-for phrases that made me rather uncomfortable. I needed a lot of courage to speak up about this. By the time I did so three months later, I did not remember the exact words the man had used. I later discovered that another employee had complained about him too.

I believe that this incident played out in this manner because people didn't take me seriously enough. Due to my diagnosis, it was felt that I must have exaggerated the circumstances. I know that this is not how every case of harassment is treated. People think that I am sometimes 'imagining' things—which might be true—but there are also times when I can clearly see through the intentions of those around me.

I urge friends and family of women diagnosed or coping with a mental disorder to treat them with care and respect. Especially in the cases of sexual assault, abuse or molestation it is difficult for women who are experiencing mental health challenges to come out and find support within the community. We must support our women in these circumstances so that their voices are not silenced.

Family Interventions

In 2016, I experienced an oddly difficult moment. I offered my brother some vanilla latte coffee that I was having, and he turned around and reminded me that it was practically 20 per cent sugar.

The words had barely left his mouth when I burst into tears, right in front of my family. I suppose it was my ego that was hurt—even my younger brother was now telling me what to do! At times such as this one, emotions and tears simply get the better of you and nothing can be done except to walk away, step back and observe them. Prior to this, it had already been pointed out to me that I should not be indulging in too many hash browns during my vacation in the Maldives. However, at that moment it was beyond me to resist the perfectly put together crisp potato.

Years later as I write this memoir I realize that my brother's intention was purely to prevent me from developing unhealthy eating habits and that was the least he could do to help me in my quest to return to a fit and healthy physique.

I know that weight loss has always been a challenge for me, especially because of some of my medications that create a larger appetite than usual. The shift in moods they produce can in turn also cause you to consume more than needed. So, I have experienced sudden losses and gains in weight and have stretchmarks to remind me of them. Yet, after the incident with my brother, I felt terribly guilty for indulging in sugar and fried potatoes because I had not truly internalized the meaning of having a healthy diet. When this desire is born from within, it is much easier to make healthy choices.

Families can also be difficult to deal with for those with conditions like bipolar because, one, the patient might be prone to anxiety and overthinking and assigning ulterior motives to the most innocent query. Two, the family might at times tend to overcompensate with its interventions in its attempt to protect you.

For most of my years in India I was treated by a family friend, a psychiatrist. When I was first diagnosed with bipolar, he was the one who flew with my father all the way to Edmonton, Alberta, to meet me and help arrive at a correct diagnosis, apart from being a strong support system to my family. In my lowest times I would have in-person appointments with the doctor and he would advise me and help me arrive at a conclusion. I eagerly looked forward to every visit I had with the doctor.

In the years that followed, I went through an extremely negative phase where I doubted everything about me, my life and even the love of my loved ones, including the doctor. I would have anxious thoughts whenever my family would talk to my psychiatrist. I would imagine a world of conspiracies being hatched against me. Now, having largely taken control of my condition, in hindsight I realize that my whole family looked out for me, and had the best intentions in mind for my mental health and well-being. At the time, though, having a rebellious streak did not help my anxieties. Even while writing this memoir, I had to go over several difficult times and revisit everything, triggering some of those anxieties all over again. However, I now had a different lens through which I could view those times.

While a family is an essential part of decision-making, it may not be that each decision they make suits you and will work out well. I guess it is the same for all decisions made independently by any person not affected by any mental health issue. Simply believing and having faith in their presence and support will go a long way. We have to look out for the real danger of infantilisation and loss of privacy that people with mental health issues are forced to face.

8

Mise en Scène

The 'Madhouse'

When my mind starts to heal, I start to remember all the things that have happened. So, I'm just going to tell you a little story.

There was a lady who had really matted hair. And there was a door which when shut separated us from the nurses. On one side, there were nurses. On our side were all patients.

And there was a clear distinction between the nurses and patients even apart from our respective locations. The nurses were well kept and clean; they smelt good, looked good and were confident about everything. And they had a tag and a card.

The card was a key to everything. They could travel anywhere they wanted, but we were trapped within those walls. I felt like a prisoner there. I wanted to leave but...

When I look back at this undated diary entry from my last stay in a mental health institution, I realize that it captures many of the emotions I have gone through when I was in one. And I have been in one many times. It is also a sobering reminder of how the system segregates us well beyond the walls of these institutions. While the segregation there is temporary, it isn't so outside. It makes me wonder: Is this the madhouse, or is it the world outside that is 'crazy'? In this chapter, I will take a moment to reflect on my experiences in the indoor variety.

Life in a hospital is mundane to some extent. Usually, there are a few extracurricular activities such as yoga, art classes and games hour for patients. We have 'passes' with which we are usually allowed to leave the facility temporarily for food, or to meet some friends and family. But much of our time is indoors, and there is only so much one can get around to doing, so boredom is common.

The doctors, in my experience, fortunately, were extremely patient, gentle and sensitive to my condition. A few nurses were rather generous, but others didn't seem to care. Which nurses enjoyed their jobs and which were not fully present and perhaps resented their work often seemed obvious to me, and I would make a guessing game of it.

The power of a truly good nurse cannot be overemphasized. I remember the graceful Sadie with her gorgeous green eyes, a stylish haircut, beautiful floral tattoos which I would gaze at, and her piercings which only added to her beauty. Her sheer kindness spoke for her true character as she always went the extra mile to make sure I was comfortable. For example, one night I was woken up as she had to administer some medication to me. She knew that I did not eat the hospital food much since I did not enjoy it. So that night she laid out a spread for me which consisted of cream cheese, butter, jam, bagels and biscuits. As simple as it may seem, to me in that moment, when I was very hungry, these snacks tasted like heaven. I will never forget the generosity of the nurse, Sadie.

Every single time I was admitted to the hospital, I thankfully had a say in the decision-making process. Nobody in my family forced me to go. My mother, however, was invariably instrumental in me deciding to go to the hospital. Seeing me go through sleepless nights, which is one of the manifestations of an episode in my case, has often taken quite a toll on my family as a whole and especially my mother. I knew this and wanted to reduce her burden by seeking help outside. Besides, I truly believed something good would come out of my institutional stays.

I did not always, like all patients, have a say in the length of my hospitalization, and it wasn't always a rosy picture on that front. Once, I even considered taking the legal route. I was aware of my rights as a patient in Canada and knew that if I happened to not agree with the doctors and their plan of action, I could present myself in a court of law and prove that I have recovered fully. But the doctor insisted that a few more days would do me good, so I finally agreed to stay a few extra days at the hospital.

There is, however, one aspect of the hospital that I loathed, and that is the isolation room. In isolation, they would tie up my wrists and feet in an attempt to calm me down. And the exposure to the many people who were all going through severe trauma in some way or the other was not always helpful. It is extremely painful to have to see older patients, especially, being dragged in. I thought to myself, I would never experience the same. But my turn surely came, and how! I had to spend over four days and nights there for a variety of reasons.

*

As confusing and intimidating as being within a facility may be, the negative aspects of the experience were heightened even further during my stay at the time of the pandemic. During my last hospitalization, I ended up being a prime suspect of the coronavirus disease. Funnily, it was I who made the mistake of raising the alarm! I was immediately put into isolation. Things were not easy even before, but with the pandemic, the issues multiplied. We weren't even permitted to leave our floor, and we were allowed only one visitor at a time. The rules were extremely stringent during this time, and in some places they still are.

The bed assigned to me had straps with buckles and metal holes to tie me down and restrict all movement in case I tried to escape. In one corner was a shiny shit pot. To top it all, as if the bed with straps and toilet seat weren't enough, there was an eye watching me from above. Each of the rooms had a camera similar to that one to ensure nothing went wrong and to prevent any disasters such as self-harm or suicide. This is what I wrote from that all-in-one compartment:

Metal buckles
Faded blue clothes
Holding me down for eternity
Struggle to escape
More pain, more bruising
Gazing at empty ceilings
Gasping for air, continuously
Shutting my eyes
Frantic for peace
Piercing shrieks
A failed attempt
To be free
A woman in white
Unties me

Despite everything, I doodled and wrote several poems when I was in there during that last stay. So, despite the loss of my sense of self, there was still some kind of order, some striving for purpose and meaning, and even when one is in that episodic state, light can shine through the darkness.

*

I am extremely open about my condition and do not feel any shame whatsoever in having been admitted into a mental health care facility several times in my life. Mine is a condition that needs extra care sometimes, and had I not admitted myself, I would only have done more harm to my health. My health is my top priority, and I think that physical and mental health go hand in hand to a large extent, for both are equally important to live a long and fruitful life.

However, since people respond to and cope differently with this news, I tend to keep it to myself sometimes. I don't discuss it mainly because I would rather not have to deal with their juvenile attitude, born directly out of stigma and ignorance. But despite these realities, there should be no shame in seeking help because everyone needs it at some point or the other, and in some way or the other. In fact, I would say it is definitely a better option to admit yourself sooner than later because when you are in an episodic state, especially in bipolar, you may spiral to a point where return becomes almost impossible, even in a short span of time. The sooner you seek help, the quicker the recovery process, and in some cases the amount of damage to your brain cells may be minimized.

It is also helpful to prepare oneself for a hospitalization. How? The answer is simple enough: carry as few material belongings as you can; stay light. But more importantly, prepare yourself mentally to heal your mind and body, and try to trust your caregivers and the entire team to help you. Without faith, it will be much harder to survive, and you may end up constantly resisting help. Lastly, be kind to others in similar positions as you, and do not judge them for their apparent mistakes or failures. Everyone has their story, just like you, and remember, you are nobody to dissect their past or find flaws in them.

*

I often wondered what brought each one of the patients to the clinic. What was their story? Being there, learning about some of their lives, sharing their plight has taught me many things and has given me a greater understanding of the world and its ways. If there is one thing my stays in hospital has taught me, it is to be accepting. And that is something that makes it all worthwhile.

For instance, I recall an elderly lady vividly. Forever smiling. Matted hair. I volunteered to help her untie the knots in her hair with coconut oil, and we connected in our own ways. Self-care and hygiene posed a challenge in the hospital, especially if the patient was elderly. However, during my several stays, I was able to connect with a lot of patients. There was one who, I was told, was aggressive and I was advised to stay away from her. However, she really liked talking to me. So I was afraid at first, but then I made the choice to talk to her. She wanted to do yoga, and as I had told her about my time in India learning yoga, she insisted we do some together. So every morning we use to do yoga asanas in the common room. Mind you, it was an intensive care unit so there were only three patients residing on that floor. Afterwards, we listened to music on YouTube.

I also introduced the patients in the unit to my YouTube channel, 'Ishaa Tanzerin', where I uploaded videos the minute I got discharged from the hospital. That was my silver lining. I was perfectly capable of dancing to a traditional song, with rhythm and beats, but as far as other aspects of life were concerned I was labelled dysfunctional. In times like these, hang on to the positive things that make you, instead of dwelling on the negative aspects such as a disorder, or mental illness that you feel is preventing you from achieving your dreams.

Here are a few lines I wrote during my time at CAMH, Canada, in July 2019:

I realized when I was in the mental hospital,
Everybody had their own journey.
And where they had arrived was a clear reflection of their journey.
Some had long journeys, some short.
Some were bruised...
But it made me realize one thing: that we are all human.
And there was no degree of separation between me and my nurses—all the way to my doctors.
They all had beating hearts, and everybody's eyes were reflective.
Some green, some grey, some brown and some black.
Eventually it led me to my own reflection.
And I thought of Gautama Buddha...
His perfection, his reflection and the embodiment of Buddhism.

9

To My Own Rescue

Let Ishaa Help Ishaa

My late uncle, Vir (Vir Papa), was a fount of wisdom. He would offer nuggets of advice that I now cling to in moments of despair. It was before his passing that he told me to be independent when it came to my mental health and to let 'Ishaa help Ishaa'. These words have made me who I am today; that, and 'knowledge leaks from everywhere'. With age and experience, I have got better at helping myself. I want to share my experiences in the hope of it being of some help to someone younger or more troubled than I. Of course, each mental health condition is different, and I'm no medical expert, so the best option is to look after yourself based on your own condition, experience, research and medical advice. You may, however, find some resonance and comfort in hearing about how I was able to help myself.

I believe that our life experiences and teachings influence and impact our world view. Be it my experiences as a child navigating my way in a boarding school at a young age, or my years of learning Indian classical dance, or even my love for children kindled through the strong bond with my younger brother Ishan—all these have made me the person I am and will impact my role as an early childhood educator. I bring strong empathy and patience to my role, a result of my lived experiences. I cannot wait to explore and engage in my role as educator as I continue to expand my learnings and worldview.

Dealing with Mood Swings

Especially when you are on medication, you often wonder if the changes in mood are due to the disorder or linked to some event in your life. It is very important to step back and ask yourself how anyone in a situation like this would have behaved. An example from personal experience is of a time when I had a break-up. I would have constant crying spells, often for six or seven days at a time. It helped me put things in perspective when my doctor reached out to me and assured me that what I was going through was completely normal under the circumstances. The important thing is to know that anything that goes down will eventually come back up and this pattern is the only constant—for everyone.

What really helped stabilize my moods to some extent was immersing myself into my hobby, dance. Doing this distracted me from my worries. I would play my brother Agni's favourite tracks on my laptop and dance my frustration away in front of the mirror.

While at Dalhousie Public School, I had proceeded to share my joy for dance with the children at the boarding school. It was magical how the positive vibrations and the energies quadrupled when I was dancing with the children. With every step they learnt, their laughter would follow, propelling me to dance with even more energy. It was as if I would throw them a ball full of energy and they would only add to it and throw it back to me. You can immerse yourself in whatever you are most passionate about—whether it is your job or a hobby—and it will be an amazingly cathartic release of stress.

Navigating Relationships

Sometimes in life, due to poor self-image, low self-esteem and lack of confidence, you may tend to date absolutely anyone under the sun who accepts you. I know I did this ever so often. Just for the sake of having someone in my life, I compromised on the quality of relationships. In such cases, the relationship is no longer about your liking something about the other person. The very idea of acceptance is enough to keep you in a relationship which wouldn't have existed if your self-image, self-esteem and confidence were in place. Self-worth is important in order to respect yourself, and going out with anyone and everyone undermines our self-worth even further and can do great harm to both the individuals involved.

The fear of rejection is ingrained in all of us. We, as a species, are designed to fear rejection. Being rejected is seen as the worst thing that could happen. And constantly being rejected by a partner can do much harm to an individual's sense of self-worth, image and self-esteem. It is important to be aware of this so the fear doesn't control us as we look for love.

Often we try everything to attract a special someone in our lives, and we go to great lengths to make a person stay without even once pausing to reflect on what it is that's so special about them. It is possible that sometimes we get so blinded with the idea of wanting to have a partner that we lose the ability to pick the right person. Sometimes we allow the other person to treat us badly until it gets to the point of no return. We wait till we start to loathe the person and then exit from the relationship.

If we taste something we do not like the taste of at the beginning, we will never take a second bite. Why can we not apply this same logic to relationships? When we do not eat anything that we do not like, why let negative people who will only harm us into our lives? This goes for both friendships and relationships. It is true that we tend to become like what we surround ourselves with. So we should be mindful, because if we surround ourselves with negativity and mediocrity, that is essentially what we will become.

All this applies to most relationships, but I have seen that if you are a woman and also have been diagnosed with bipolar disorder, others often tend to take advantage of your situation. The purpose is not to point fingers at anyone, but simply to make others in similar situations be aware of this possibility. It is important to protect and prioritize yourself in a relationship.

Today, I would probably urge any potential partner of mine to read this memoir. I'm kidding, but in all seriousness, I would surely be frank and open about everything so he is prepared for what can possibly happen.

A piece of advice I would like to give partners who are with people diagnosed with mental health issues is to make sure your partner gets the appropriate counselling they need from a therapist, as well as proper medical attention from a psychiatrist. It is not always necessary for you to be part of the process, but if you feel you can handle it, don't stop yourself from learning about participating in your partner's recovery. Having had the illness myself, and looking back, I sometimes think it would have been nice to have had my ex take part in my healing process; it would have been a good support system. But then again, you should always stick to what works for you, because sometimes being completely engaged in the recovery process may get overwhelming—for you or your partner.

With our generation in general, I feel we lack love and compassion for each other as fellow humans. Many a times there is a huge amount of research that goes into how to be a good lover, but this mainly means how to be good in bed. But whatever happened to the basic human qualities of dignity, honesty, love and compassion? Whatever happened to the pursuit of being a good human? Instead, we fall prey to a cycle that will not let us find love: We get our hearts broken by someone, and we then proceed to do exactly the same thing to another human being we interact with in future. To protect ourselves in relationships, we must watch out for these cycles and break out of them as soon as we see them forming.

Some people say that the goal of life is to be happy in the present moment. Yet we are so regretful of the past and eager about the future that our present slips away like sand through our palms. It is an easy concept to understand that the present is all we have, but to actually internalize it and apply it in our day-to-day living takes great awareness and understanding about the universe.

Ill-treatment of Persons with Mental Health Conditions: How to Handle It

I strongly believe that in order to treat a patient, we must first treat them as the humans they are, and not as lab rats. Experimenting on a patient, or using different medicines and techniques without their consent, is unacceptable. The worst remedy for a person with hyperactivity, or who is suicidal, is sending them to what I would like to call an isolation 'chamber'. It is a pathetic remedy, and it only makes matters worse. Who among us would like our hands and feet tied up tightly while we lie on a cement bed with a dirty mattress? Even animals have rights and ought to be treated better in this day and age.

We, as a society, must find ways to avoid harsh treatments, which are only a festering ground for trauma. They hinder growth or improvement and scar a patient for life. Once we develop alternative treatments, one wouldn't view a mental hospital negatively but rather as a place that facilitates rebirth.

In Canada we have the Personal Health Information Protection Act (PHIPA) 2004 to protect the rights of patients. I want to describe at length *why* this Canadian Act came into existence, and not *what* constitutes it. It is the right of any patient—and as in my case, any mental health patient—to keep their diagnosis to themselves and not disclose it to any employer or educational institute. If it is indeed shared with a doctor, or an employer, they are bound by law to not share the information with anyone. I believe this Act provides patients with self-respect, care and agency in relation to their condition. It is extremely important that a patient be respected, but it is even more important that a patient not be disrespected or mistreated due to their diagnosis.

It is always a good idea to research the law of the land where you reside. To remain one step ahead, having knowledge of all the laws in relation to health and mental health, especially if you are a patient or a loved one of a patient, will always work in your favour.

I began to appreciate this in a job at an early childhood centre in Mumbai. A close member of the family had pointed out that it was my responsibility to disclose to any employer that I had bipolar disorder, else the employers could hold that against me at a later date when they found out. This affected me a lot, and finally I quit the job. I do not blame anyone for this simply because people in India do not have enough information about mental health advocacy. There are a lot of grey areas in this which is detrimental to a person dealing with such issues. In the West, at least no one is forced to reveal their condition to their employer or an educational institute, even if they choose to ask for accommodations.

Another related topic is the concept of accommodations in the West. With a doctor's note or a consultation from a college / university counsellor, students can have their needs considered and avail of certain 'accommodations' that help them cope. If they need extra time to complete a test or an assignment, it will be provided for appropriately. I hope in all other parts of the world, not just in India, this practice is adopted for the mental well-being of all students.

Dealing with Hallucinations—Minor and Major

Once, due to a mistake in the dosage of medications, I experienced minor hallucinations. I was completely aware at the time that they were hallucinations, as I was warned about it before. In retrospect, I now understand that this occurs only when I am extremely bothered, stressed or worn out. For me, when this happens, I tend to see lights and colours in all different shapes, sizes and patterns.

When experiencing hallucinations, it is important to step back, disconnect and constantly remind yourself that what you are seeing does not exist. What helped me, and perhaps the best comparison I can make is this: a hallucination is probably like a boggart (a reference to Harry Potter, where a boggart is something that takes the form of your deepest fears), and the only real way to tackle it is to think of happy thoughts and memories. For me what helped the most in that moment was reminding myself that the colours were not real and did not exist, or rather that they did so only in my mind. We as humans fear the unknown; so probably the first time the hallucinations occur, they would be terrifying for anyone experiencing them. However, once we acknowledge their existence and remind ourselves what they really are, dealing with the rest is a piece of cake.

This same concept can be applied to bipolar episodes. When someone experiences them for the first time ever, one can get carried away and not have full control over one's emotions. However, our minds are very powerful even in sickness, and sometimes it is possible to be aware of our emotions while being sick.

During my episode after my separation, when I was taken to the hospital, the doctor entered, looked at me and my mom and asked, 'Who is the patient?' He found it hard to think that I was the patient because I was sitting there casually, with my purse hung over my shoulder, knowing well that I was there for treatment. I would say things like, 'Doctor, I am in a mixed episode now, right? Because I feel happy and feel like crying at the very same time.' And he would reply, 'Yes.' I am talking purely from my experience and I am no certified doctor, but the point here is that knowing the possible chance of episodes and what exactly they consist of is the first step to preventing your mind from losing complete awareness.

Coping with Psychosomatic Pains

The truth is that when it comes to it, many of our problems are really all in our minds. If you are in mental pain and are feeling miserable, chances are it will manifest in your body too—whether in the form of a life-threatening illness (compounded over several years), a migraine or imaginary bodily sensations. Having said that, these experiences must not be dismissed as non-existent, since they are the lived reality of the patients.

In my case, with bipolar, sometimes I have experienced heightened bodily sensations that don't actually exist. For example, when you are extremely stressed, your mind may take full control and force you to believe that every sensation in your body is due to something other than itself. I experienced this when I had a pregnancy scare. The very next day I imagined pains in parts of my stomach, which to me were very prominent but whether they truly existed or not, I do not know, for the doctor could not identify any particular cause. Having said this, I put my fear aside in order to be able to cope with work. Once, I had a dance performance and I had to do it despite what I was experiencing. In that moment I realized that when you truly put your mind to something you are passionate about, your mind is diverted and you can momentarily stop thinking about the stressors in life.

Living with the Side Effects of Medication

Due to a high dose of medication, sometimes we experience sluggishness and lethargy. Experiencing lethargy can be extremely challenging. There is a slowness in speech and motion. Everything feels like it is playing out in slow motion. Since I have experienced this, I know that it has to be consciously fought against. It is very easy to give in to the feeling of wanting to sleep over and over again. The constant desire to close my eyes is in a way an escape from truly living. It is merely a coping mechanism, but is often viewed by others as a cowardly act.

One day spent in bed doesn't make a difference; however, when repeated numerous times, it can sometimes reach a stage where it is almost impossible to return to the rigour of life.

One tactic to help counter lethargy is going for a long shower. This wakes up our body and ignites the mind. Another effective method is to go for a long walk or run, so that endorphins that can help counter the effects of the medicine are released.

Being Sexually Active While on Medication (For Women)

It is very important to check with your doctor whether the medications prescribed will have an impact on a possible pregnancy. Having to undergo an abortion because of abnormalities in a pregnancy can then be pre-empted. Of course, at the end of the day the onus is on the doctors to declare all potential side effects, but it doesn't hurt to be aware of your own condition and exercise greater control in the matter given that we do not live in an ideal world.

I still remember an incident from the time when I was married. I was told by my ex-husband's boss's wife, who was also a doctor, that one of the medicines I was taking at the time (valproic acid) would be harmful if I planned to have kids anytime soon. I recall vaguely that I overreacted and flushed all my medicines down the toilet. It resulted in a string of violent abuses when my ex-husband found out about it. I wanted to be prescribed medicines that were safe for me to take if we ever wanted to give birth to a child. But as soon as I stopped taking them, I started slipping; I would stay awake for nights at a stretch. I could not have a proper sleep cycle back then and was irregular with my medications. I really, really, really didn't want to go to a mental health facility, but I did want to protect my chances of having a baby. There was an absence of a clear-cut communication between me and my ex-husband about health precautions, especially in my particular case since I was on psychotic medication. I was absolutely and utterly paranoid about what could possibly happen to a potential pregnancy with the valproic acid I was consuming on a daily basis.

Building a Support System

Being tied up or sent to an isolation room for a whole day are experiences that rarely find sympathy from people. Only close family, therapists, nurses and doctors can truly understand what a person with a mental health condition goes through. I would bottle up my feelings inside and never tell anyone that I was in search of true acceptance from a partner or a friend. For this reason, I would advise that certain things be shared only with professionals or those we trust completely. There is no need to share everything with everyone. Keeping a close circle of caregivers who may or may not understand but are actually willing to go all the way in supporting us or lending us a listening ear to help lighten the burden is more rewarding.

Those closest to you will always show you the mirror and tell you the truth of how you are coping. Sometimes it is of great help to receive this feedback, however shocking, from family and friends, so that if you aren't doing well, not only can you spot it quickly but you can also find support to handle your misery. The feedback you receive can also be translated and conveyed to your therapists, counsellors and psychiatrists. At times this process of hearing what others have to say may hurt, but it is important to take the constructive criticism in such a way that it doesn't hinder but rather helps in the healing process.

Disclosing Your Illness: When, How and Whom to Trust

One of the many dilemmas for a person diagnosed with bipolar disorder, or for that matter any other mental health condition, is when exactly to disclose your diagnosis to the person you are close to. The answer varies and would look different for each person and each relationship. However, it is important that the person dating you needs to first see you for the person you are and get to know your personality in totality before you disclose the fact that you have a mental health condition.

If the first thing your partner finds out about you is a mental health condition, chances are that he/she will begin to make judgements based on that. Each action and each spoken word will be viewed in the light of their perception of your condition. I am not saying that one should hide one's illness; in fact, it is imperative that one does the opposite—offer full disclosure. However, it is equally important to do so at the right time.

Being honest may of course come in handy in the event of any health crisis where the support of your partner is crucial.

Choosing Company and Work

I have noticed from my experience that there seem to be three types of people in relation to responses to disclosures on mental health. In the first category are those who try their best to understand the condition. They ask questions and listen to the answers but finally, despite all their efforts, may fail to truly understand what is going on, especially after hearing detailed accounts of depressive or manic episodes.

The second category comprises those who try to understand what the patient is going through and succeed in understanding and empathizing with the individual. They have perhaps faced mental health issues themselves, have witnessed it in their own families, or are simply better equipped to empathize.

The last, and probably my least favourite category, consists of people who refuse to understand mental health issues. They ignore the situation at hand and pretend that the problem is non-existent or, even worse, unimportant. This may sometimes be due to their own problems with mental health or those of loved ones, or they may simply be unable to grasp what is unfolding before them. I do not blame them, but when I run into this category of people, I tend to immediately write them off my list of people to be friends with in order to ensure that I do not end up hurting myself in the bargain.

It is now a well-known fact that stress does trigger or instigate episodes in people with bipolar disorder. This is why it is crucial that people with this disorder choose their friend circles and partners wisely and carefully. The physical and emotional abuse I experienced in my short-lived marriage triggered my episodes, resulting in three hospitalizations and rehabs over a span of nine months.

It is also important to choose an occupation which comes along with the least amount of stress. And if it is a high-stress job that is your calling, it is important not to take things too seriously.

Many a times people diagnosed with bipolar rebel and want to only do the things that require them to do late nights, such as jobs in journalism or media. However, we need to prioritize our health and work around our health limitations. I have come across several people with bipolar who refuse to come to terms with the early nights rule in particular. We are all creatures of habit, and once we get habituated to early nights, it will come effortlessly. Besides, late nights are not only bad for people with bipolar; the idea that one can be sleep-drunk is well known and has been proven. Being in this state is equivalent to having a certain percentage of alcohol in your system and it prohibits you from functioning optimally.

Staying Positive About People and Life

It is the easiest thing in life to develop doubt and let negativity take over your thought processes. If we give in to all the muck and negative influences in the world, it would be like a beautiful lotus drowning in the muddy lake, instead of it standing out despite the dirt that surrounds it.

In life we lose faith in people because ever so often we come across people who cheat us, whether it be in personal or professional relationships. My father told me recently that no matter how many negative experiences he has faced in life with people, it has never once wavered his faith in humanity. It is crucial for us as human beings to have this faith because if we lose it, we will become miserable beings who will constantly attract additional negativity in our lives. The key is to ignore the bad that people do and focus on the good. There is enough goodness in the world for all of us. The reason we don't notice it is because we are obsessed with the negativity and fail to recognize the miracles in our lives.

*

We all know that many companies have helpline numbers where you can register complaints. But how often do you see people using this line to express their gratitude for good service or experience? Our very first reaction is to find faults or mistakes with people. Rarely do we notice the niceness in people.

Below is an email I sent to a company praising their employee:

> This email is [written] with the pure intent to compliment Ms Pushpam Singh; I feel she has tremendous people skills and is intelligent and sensitive towards her clients. Having interacted with her briefly, I thought it my duty to inform you that I was very happy with [her] commitment towards making me feel comfortable and satisfied.

Most people write complaints but very few write compliments. We have an attitude of entitlement. We think we deserve the best, and if we get it, well and good, but if we don't, it is all because of the problems that lie in this universe.

There is never a guidebook that leads us to the solution that is within ourselves. So, we look outward for blame and justifications, and end up making accusations. The bitter truth is that we are only in control of ourselves. And if we do not realize this, people will never take us seriously.

Exploring the Creative Process as Therapy

My mother was making a documentary film on mental health for her Master of Fine Arts (MFA) thesis. As long as I have known, my mother has always used her passion for film-making to deal with her demons—whether it be a film about immigrant youth experiences featuring me or a biographical documentary on her late father who was also a film-maker. So, it only made sense that when I was diagnosed, my mother took to the camera to film, record, analyse and critique our lives. Our relationship took a turn for the better when I too began to share my writings with her, and she in turn began to capture our journey on film. This was a breakthrough moment in the way we viewed each other, and we realized that we both were in this together, so neither of us needed to deal with it alone. We recognized that there were others going through the same or similar trauma of mental health conditions, and we wanted to reach out to them. This positivity prompted us to work on this film, which was titled *Unfinished*, together.

Below is a transcript of a conversation between us from the film, which may offer clarity on my experience of the therapeutic nature of the creative process:

S: Tell me, what do you think this film should be about?

Me: I think one of the main topics this film should be about is defining what 'normal' is and why everyone is so obsessed with being judged by society about [the] little-little things and [why] everyone tries so hard to follow a certain way of living and to conform to society's norms and values instead of deciding for themselves what to do in life.

S: Aren't we all on a continuum? Aren't we all sometimes, out of … have an experience which is, out of character? We all behave sometimes like we're out of character!

Me: I think what we have to do is, we have to make peace with the fact that there will be good days and there will be bad days. And there will be highs, and there will be lows. And we need to come to terms with the fact that, you know what, it's okay. There's nothing wrong with that. If we realize that there's nothing wrong with that, we will take pride in whatever happens to us, because we won't judge ourselves then. We will be able to view ourselves in the mirror with pride and say, *You know what? It's okay*. [This will be] especially [good] for people who are taking medication … I might be on meds, but I'm a human first, and that comes first. Nobody can [or rather should] judge me [based] on the fact that I'm taking meds for the brain, for instance. Because people [do] judge you on that; I think it's very unfair to the person because it messes with the way he views himself, the way society views him, the way his parents view him. ... It warps the whole sense of the identity that the person has. I have noticed that many people who have bipolar say, 'Oh you know what ya...' [*sic*] ... Instead of saying, 'My name is Ishaa Chopra', for example, I say, 'I'm a bipolar patient', but you know what? That's not me. I am a person first, I'm a human first. I am Ishaa. I have a personality separate from bipolar, and that does not define me. Yes, it's a part of me, it's an ugly part of me, but it doesn't define me.

S: Why do you say ugly? I think it's beautiful at times.

Me: I think the only reason that I say ugly [is] because it sometimes brings out the worst in me. Some things that, may be at some points in time, I don't have control over; but then again, one message that I would definitely like to give out to people is [this]: When you know, for instance, [that] a car has run over your leg, and you know you have to stay in bed for some time, you have to put certain medicines on it. Why can't we treat our brain [I mean mind] the same way? If people know, for instance, [that] you can't have alcohol when you're on meds, [and] you can't have late nights, why can't people just follow these things? It's not very difficult; I've never been drunk in my entire life; and trust me I don't think

I'm missing out—you forget everything anyway when you get drunk. I have ... the advantage of not remembering everything.

S: But even when you have your highs in bipolarity that's like being drunk, in a sense, isn't it?

Me: Yeah ... Definitely, you're high, you don't remember anything afterwards. I think maybe that's a good thing in a way, because our brain always, no matter if it's sick or not sick, it works in our favour, so it wipes out the ugly memories. And I think that even works for people who are not bipolar patients; I'm sure a lot of research has gone into it ... [If] a child is having a bad childhood [*sic*], for instance, our brain will unconsciously wipe out whatever is negative, and we just don't want to remember that. We, as humans ... we want to hang on to the positive things.

In Lieu of a Conclusion

I had a really engaging conversation on the topics discussed here during an interview in January 2022 with a close friend, Susan (name changed in the interest of privacy). She has also been diagnosed with bipolar disorder. I reproduce an excerpt below for readers interested in knowing the views of others like me.

Ishaa: What are the repercussions on relationships of having a mental health diagnosis such as bipolar disorder?

Susan: I think a lot of people are scared of bipolar, they don't know much about it or have had bad experiences with it, so I think bringing that into the fold is a bit challenging. It really depends on the person you are with and their comfort level. So, just in general, navigating the world of dating and even just interpersonal relationships like friendships and stuff can be challenging because of having a disorder. It makes it harder.

Ishaa: Do you feel sometimes you know immediately who your friends are and those friendships stay forever, or is it hard to even make those friends?

Susan: I don't find it hard to make friends. I've actually found that the friendships I have where talking about these kinds of subjects is not quite as common are pleasant in their own way too. Sometimes it can be really heavy talking about bipolar. I enjoy both friendships where it's on the table to talk about [bipolar] and also friendships where we communicate about a variety of topics.

Ishaa: You were talking about interpersonal relationships. Is there anything that impacted your relationship with your family members or did it not have any effect at all?

Susan: No, it definitely had an effect and I think there are still questions that I have for my family members about how my manic episodes have affected things. It definitely had a negative effect, I would say, with relationships with my family members in ways that I didn't really expect. How could I have known? I think there is a lot to talk about in this domain but it is also a very sensitive topic.

Ishaa: It has affected my relationships with my mother and my father. My father, for instance, is in another continent and the only access with him is through voice/video calls. I can meet him in person only when I travel to India or when he comes here. This in the normal course would sound like the reality of many others but can be an arduous climb for a person striving with bipolar or any mental health issue. And my mom got very emotionally and professionally involved in my life because she made the film on mental health, *Unfinished*, with me as a subject. It took a high emotional toll on her because watching and rewatching, editing and re-editing the content made her extremely aware of my condition and that kind of affected our relationship. She was aware that if I fell sick and anything happened to me, it would have a grave impact on everyone in the family, including my teenage brother, Ishan, who, when he was applying for universities, mentioned my mental health as one of the challenges he had to overcome. It has repercussions that are all-round. It is not just about me, it's about all my loved ones too.

Susan: That's tough. Sorry to hear that.

Ishaa: As far as relationships go, you are right. It's really hard to find a partner [who] will accept you completely, and I think more than accepting, it is also a partner who will understand you completely. Accepting is important, but understanding the condition is also very important to me, and many people do not understand it and cannot wrap their head around it. And some people try but they don't get what it's about and what they can do to make it better, and usually they just make it worse.

Susan: That's tough. You need to find someone who really makes an effort. For example, I was with someone for five years and the best he could do was [read] the first two or three pages of a document that I gave him that summarized bipolar, and he really had no clue. He wasn't making an effort to try and understand what the illness is and how to deal with it. That was uncool. I don't particularly feel like he was the best guy in general; that was my mistake … selecting such a weird guy. In general, being with someone who is understanding and kind and has all of those positive qualities becomes even more important when you have a mental health condition, and it becomes more clear and almost dangerous to think of all the kind of situations you can get into if the partner isn't safe.

Ishaa: Would you consider being with someone who has a mental health condition themselves?

Susan: Yeah, probably, I think I would be. We need to recognize the challenges that come with it, because I have dealt with it myself. I wouldn't cut someone out just because they have a mental health condition, although it is hard.

Ishaa: Speaking of mental health conditions, how long do you wait until you disclose to your potential partner that you have bipolar disorder?

Susan: That's a tough question. I would say not until a month.

Ishaa: A month?

Susan: Like a month of serious dating, of really getting to know each other, feeling like there could be something serious. But speaking of my experience with dating in the past, it has come up a lot earlier because I always had the tendency of wanting to be upfront pretty early on in the relationship. It depends on the guy, but I think in my ideal situation I wouldn't let the guy know too early on so that it gives the guy a chance to get to know me inside out before making a decision. How about you?

Ishaa: I usually disclose almost immediately. However, I know it is a mistake on my part because usually when I do, the guys vanish into thin air. I was talking to this guy who studied at Stanford; he still talks to me but hasn't made a move yet to meet or date. Some people don't really understand but still they think it is okay, without looking too much into it. This is because the irony of this illness [is that] when anyone talks to us, we are more than normal or the usual. We aren't like manic or depressive when we are talking to someone, so it is really hard for somebody to fathom that there may be something wrong with us because there is such a difference in behaviour from when we are sick and when we are well.

Susan: I think people want to stay by [your side] when everything is fine, and when things aren't well they have a tendency to give up and vanish.

Ishaa: What is your method of dealing with bipolar or your go-to thing to prevent episodes?

Susan: My sleep schedule and cycle is something that I keep a track of. Going to bed at the same time every night. I try and stay healthy by keeping a good diet and exercising so that endorphins are released. I have monthly meetings with my psychiatrist and I am fully honest with him. In the past I tried to manage my own medication which is not such a good idea. All these things keep me going.

10

Accept, Grow, Learn

Lessons for a Lifetime

My first episode had me running away from the country I lived in and loved so much: Canada. My second episode ruined my reputation as a dancer and left me fleeing from Pune, a city I had long been a resident of. My third episode had me on the run again, away from my new-found family and friends in Germany, which I left to return to India.

Seeing this pattern now, I realize that however far one attempts to flee, there is no place to escape from your own mind and thoughts. Wherever you go, your brain goes with you, your mind accompanies you. I hope one day I have the courage to face my ghosts. Once I arrive at a balance, no matter where I am, I won't have the urge to exile myself to a different world.

I sometimes used to think that perhaps if I was regular with my medications and had prioritized my health, my life would have turned out differently. However, wishful thinking serves no purpose. The lines from Max Ehrrman's poem 'Desiderata' describes my feelings aptly: 'Whether or not it is clear to you, no doubt the universe is unfolding as it should. Therefore, be at peace with God, whatever you conceive Him to be.'

I would like to now share some of my reflections about acceptance, which I have arrived at after all these experiences.

Acceptance of Others Unlike Us and Ourselves

> 'Serenity comes when you trade expectations for acceptance.'
>
> —Gautama Buddha

If we function from a place of acceptance, most labels in the world would cease to exist. If we accepted women loving women, men loving men, all the derogatory terms used to categorize same-sex relationships would cease to exist. Similarly, if we accepted certain behaviours that stem from genes or behaviours rooted in a person's upbringing, we wouldn't need to single out some people and categorize them as different, like we do now.

Most labels, especially in mental health, arise because of some notion of abnormality which is defined by society to be wrong or not in sync with 'perfection'. But who determines what is 'normal' and what isn't? The term 'normal' is in itself harmless, but to imply that it is the state that everyone should identify with is assuming something that is not only impossible, but unfair to the minority.

If we believe in a God or a universal power, we can certainly reflect on why certain people are born a particular way, but how can we give ourselves the power to exclude, shame, punish and ignore those different from us? How do we as a society hold that right? The problem lies with us and our inability to accept other people and their personal choices. To rob someone of their freedom, or to make them live in fear forever for the rest of their lives, just so we are comfortable, is more than cruel.

We all have our own normal. Everything is 'normal' and acceptable until there is a conflict of interest, such as when we witness something that goes against our beliefs, values or morals. What is normal and acceptable to one person may not be so to another. This point can be extended to a larger group of people and, finally, society as a whole. We should embrace this gracefully, because we are unique as individuals and we owe it to our DNA. How monotonous life would be if we were all the same! Difference of opinion is the only thing common to all of us. The rest is academic.

Once we come to accept this and question 'normalcy', we will also learn to accept ourselves. Each one of us is worthy of acceptance, and we must start with ourselves. We owe ourselves love and respect, and we must give ourselves our due because if we don't, we won't notice the difference when someone disrespects us. Self-love is of utmost importance.

Accepting Ourselves Despite Others

I think it is crucial that we as individuals enjoy our own company and love ourselves. We undermine the importance of this. Today I have reached a point where I can be by myself for hours at a stretch without going crazy. I can do things I enjoy alone—listening to music, watching movies, dancing, working out or cooking. But this was not always so.

Even when the basic needs of the human race, such as nutrition and shelter, are met with, we are still so smitten with misery. Some may say it's because we as humans are destined for greater things—we are not animals, thanks to the complexities of the human brain. But the ultimate truth is that in this quest for greater things, we end up surrounding ourselves with negativity and pain.

It is important for us to filter out the content we let into our systems as much as possible, including news, music, movies, television and web series. Every medium affects us on some level or the other, and we tend to pick up on these signals consciously or unconsciously. This is true especially for children, because what they pick up at an early age can later influence their adult behaviour and life choices. This is also true for adults and that's easy to forget sometimes.

Another increasingly crucial concept to consider is the mirage that a high number of friends or followers on social media equals the quality of friendships one has. We are in the age of loneliness where people find it easier to connect with strangers over chat than to meet someone in-person and connect through conversations and eye-contact. If we actually try and make a conscious effort to connect with friends, we could possibly prevent isolation, mental and physical illnesses, and increase our happiness quotient. The more we connect and share memorable positive moments with our friends, the higher the chances of survival in this wilderness called life. We are in this together, and in supporting each other, whether it is a family, friend or stranger, we increase the frequency of positive moments, significantly reducing widespread fear and anxiety in this generation.

We often compare ourselves to others and think that there is always something missing in life. It seems that the more we get, the more we want, and as we crave for more, we feel we have less of everything, ultimately creating a constant cycle of pain. In her song '*Soak up the sun*', Sheryl Crow wisely said: 'It's not having what you want / It's wanting what you've got.' These were the thoughts that crossed my mind when I once saw a woman from an affluent background breaking into tears. At first glance, one couldn't have imagined that she would have anything to complain about, but on noticing her tears it occurred to me—it doesn't matter how much or how little material possessions we have in life, the pursuit of happiness is something we all struggle with at some point or the other. It does seem to me though that the higher we move in the social hierarchy, the more things we tend to find fault with. I believe that the lesser we have, the simpler our lives become. Hence the saying: simple living, high thinking. The more we accumulate—thoughts and material things—and the more people we attach ourselves to, the greater the chances of getting emotionally scarred.

I do not mean that we shouldn't work on cultivating meaningful relationships. I simply mean that we must keep a safe distance and not get so carried away by anyone or anything that we lose the ultimate focus in life: our sanity and peace of mind. Much too often we give others the power to control our happiness. At the end of the day, it is all about balance. It might be a hoary cliché, but joy and sorrow are indeed two sides of the same coin.

The key is not giving others the power to control our moods. True strength and power lie in our ability to be self-reliant—emotionally and financially—so we do not let external factors influence our internal functioning. The ultimate truth is that we are born alone and we die alone, but as humans we cannot accept it. Once we accept this, everything will become easy because we will know that not only are material things not going to stay forever, but even the relationships that we form over the years will eventually fade away.

We are all part of a larger picture, and the canvas of life changes constantly.

As Mitch Albom puts it beautifully in his book *Tuesdays with Morrie*:

> *Life is like a train journey.*
> *We all have to get off at some point.*
> *Coming into life isn't our prerogative and when to leave is not either.*
> *We come and go and we are just like the droplets of an ocean,*
> *Coming to the end and hitting the shore.*
> *The realization strikes us that it's all going to be over*

When an ingenious droplet says, 'No, no, don't you understand? We are all part of the same ocean!'

Accepting Things Beyond Control

Many a times in life we imagine a particular future in our head, whether it is sharing a future with a partner, or having a particular job with regular promotions. This causes us a lot of misery when something doesn't go according to plan because in our minds we have already experienced the future we imagined for ourselves, and when the opportunity of living the experience is snatched away from us, it feels like being thrown into a stormy ocean without a life jacket. Hence, although it is easier said than done, life would become less stressful and we would be able to take everything that unfolds with a pinch of salt if we didn't count on our self-written destinies as much as we do. We cannot decide our future for ourselves because nothing goes according to our plans, as much as we would like to deny this fact. However, since it is human nature to fear the unknown, we strive to transform the unknown into something known in our own minds.

Nurture vs Nature

I have now started recording all my moods using photographs. The good, the bad and the ugly. What this tells me is that when I'm well, I'm beautiful. When I'm sick, I feel fat and ugly. And when I'm extremely low and depressed, my defence mechanism tells me to prove it to the entire universe that I'm fine.

Science or religion, mathematics or art, STEAM or dance, or even A or B ... It is all part of the same alphabet, having different representations. For me, these equations translate into the 'yin-yang' philosophy. Without one, the other cannot exist.

When I see the world through the lens of a scientist or an artist, it enables me to analyse, interpret and observe diligently my own healing process. It is as if I would be healing a child or anyone else.

This logic, if applied to ourselves, involves saying: I am not alone, my inner strength and conscience are with me. I am with myself.

All it means is that I am opening up to my own thoughts, but at the same time I am becoming aware of exactly how I am feeling. Which is why when I am low, I know I will be high next, and when I am high, I know I will be low next.

'Kill Your Parents'

At first, the idea of 'killing your parents' is the hardest thing to comprehend. I know it was for me too. 'What do you mean?' I questioned a friend, Vaibhav Narula, who first mentioned it to me. He is a research student and explained the concept to me at length.

'We must be our own person and detach ourselves from the images of our parents,' he said. Not only do we need to detach ourselves; we need to remember to not take every opinion to heart. This is the only path of evolution, the only way we can ensure that the next generation's intellect and experience would be a positive addition to humanity. We must embrace our own individuality without letting our genetics define us. We are more than what we are made of, scientifically speaking; we must not be mere clones of the previous generation or try to emulate our parents consciously or subconsciously.

We must avoid blindly listening to society and societal norms and values so we can make up our own minds and think for ourselves, whether that be for choosing a particular religious practice, scientific practices, or even politics.

Although education teaches us a lot, seldom does it teach us to think for ourselves. We often rely on our parents and society to make important life choices for us. Later, we play the blame game. But the truth is that after a certain point we must take all responsibility for our actions. This is the hard but honest truth.

This applies especially to those of us who ascribe any kind of label to ourselves. Without realizing it, we sometimes let a particular ideology make decisions for us as opposed to arriving at our own opinions. Why let an ideology dictate our thought processes blindly without internalizing the true essence of what it really means?

It is very important that we as individuals exercise our individuality; the only way we can do that is when we free ourselves from the shackles of society.

Fighting Mental Health Stigma: Towards Acceptance

While we have evolved considerably as a society, why does so much stigma still surround mental health? People with mental disorders often have to face a mountain of rejection at the hands of their family, friends and even personal relationships. There may be several reasons for this.

Many times, out of plain ignorance, some family members live in denial; they do not want to accept that there are people with mental health conditions present in their homes. Mental health conditions, most often, are seen in a bad light, as it is sometimes impossible to avoid episodes. This is true to some extent with disorders such as bipolar which may involve the recurrence of cyclic episodes of mania and/or depression in a patient's lifetime. And sometimes the solution is out of our control. For instance, recovery may depend on a combination of medicines, frequent counselling sessions and appropriate sleep–wake cycles, and it may not always be possible to access or maintain them.

In some cases, mental health issues run in the family in the form of inter-generational trauma or genetics, and thus some family members have dealt with them long enough, leading them to deny their existence in the next generation out of sheer fear and exhaustion.

My way of coping with stigma is to think that I should never give in to it. By telling myself that I am not good enough for the world around me, or that I am lesser than others, I end up creating a divide between the outer world and myself, and this makes it even more difficult to break down the barriers. The problem lies with how our society views behavioural problems linked with mental health conditions. If we tell ourselves that it is no different than any other illness or disorder, and take the required medication and any other necessary precautions or steps to heal or cope, we will all make our lives much easier.

The truth is: A disorder such as bipolar is a problem only if you view it and treat it as such. I would like to put it simply: Whether it is a problem or not, either way you are right! So, it is a problem only if we make it out to be one, and it really isn't if we take it with a pinch of salt. Advances in medical science today have provided us with ample tools to cope with this or any other disorder. It should not be taken lightly, but following some simple rules such as having early nights, and staying away from alcohol, drugs and coffee (especially in the second half of the day) can take us a long way in many cases. If we follow these simple rules, we can lead regular, productive and extremely satisfying lives, just like most others.

Despite this outlook, I have had to face my share of stigma and discrimination. I had once applied for a job at an early childhood education centre, a daycare, and I got the job. There was an interview where they asked me extremely personal and intrusive questions, such as, 'How long were you in an abusive relationship for?' and 'Why are you extra close with the infants in the room? Why don't you spend equal time with children of all ages?' They even went to the extent of asking me, 'Did you ever go to a rehab or are you taking any medications?' This was literally the last straw. I withdrew my application for the job and moved on.

I have already discussed various instances where I faced rejection in my personal life. It is not easy to have a stable romantic life when there is so much stigma attached to your condition, and so little awareness.

I truly owned my illness only at a much later stage in life, mainly after my divorce. The experience of being a survivor of domestic violence propelled me to speak up, and once I learnt to do so, I also became an advocate for mental health and decided to help eradicate the stigmas associated with it. Prior to my marriage, I was mostly stable and I did not have many episodes; afterwards, I was pushed to the limit and my brain surrendered. I could not take the abuse.

The worst thing for someone with bipolar disorder who particularly struggles with mania and hypo-mania is overstimulation. This could be anything that could possibly trigger someone who is prone to the illness. The best way to combat it is with sleep, rest and regular sleep–wake cycles which coincide with the time that a patient takes their medications.

Ground Rules for Life

Before concluding this chapter, I want to offer the best advice that I can share with anyone going through a similar ordeal. Here are a few ground rules:

1. Early nights: Sleeping early is extremely crucial for mental well-being. Sleep cycles and mood cycles are both cycles and are hence controlled by the same region of the brain. Therefore, if we disturb our sleep cycle, our mood cycle will also go for a toss. This is but a simple explanation. I feel this is true for everyone and not only people diagnosed with bipolar.

2. Regular medication: It is important to take medicines daily and at the right time so that they can be most effective. If you are on medication, however, it is imperative that you share a transparent relationship with your psychiatrist/counsellor. A psychiatrist prescribes medication. Therefore, it is critical that a patient seek a psychiatrist's advice on medication.

3. Regular meetings with a psychiatrist: If you are on medication for bipolar disorder, it is important to keep meeting your doctor so that he can assess you. It is possible that the doctor may want to make changes in the dosage depending on how you are doing. It is also very important to discuss any side effects of the prescribed drugs.

4. Regular counselling sessions: Sometimes, it is impossible to be the proper judge of your own behaviour. It proves to be beneficial if you involve your counsellors and share absolutely everything with them. Also, it is important that they respect confidential information and not share your details with any family members if you do not wish them to. The sooner you can function as an individual without involving others in the process, the better it is. In addition, too many opinions and too much advice can ruin things. It is best to filter out advice and only approach those you trust for it.

5. Daily exercise: It is now a well-proven fact, supported by many doctors and scientists alike, that regular physical activity releases endorphins and causes a natural high. In my personal experience, the days I dance for long periods of time, the other humdrum tasks become easier to complete. Dr Soumitra Pathare, a doctor who treated me while I lived in Pune, once told me that 90 per cent of our lives are boring and filled with routine, and only the other 10 per cent is exciting. If this is true, for us to survive the majority of the time, it is crucial that we remain active and eradicate sluggish behaviour that both stem from and result in the blues.

6. Healthy diet: This suggestion is the least followed, but ultimately, we are what we eat. Apart from eating, especially if you are on drugs such as lithium

which consists of salts mainly, it is very important that you flush out your system with large amounts of water to remain healthy. A healthy lifestyle includes a good diet, which involves excluding things such as caffeine, sugar and fried foods. It is always a good idea to follow a diet designed by a nutritionist, but if you cannot do that, just make a lifestyle choice and decide to eat healthy, flushing out your system with as much water as you can.

7. Avoid caffeine/alcohol: It is important to do this as it tends to stop certain medications from working and may interfere with the healing process by making the person consuming it hyper. Consumption of alcohol is the worst challenge many patients face every day. It is detrimental for bipolar patients on medication because, much like caffeine, it alters the balance of moods and causes mood swings and triggers episodes.

11

Finding a Voice

Notes to Myself

The year Covid struck, I was in and out of the hospital. While the world was facing a pandemic, I was struggling with my own illness. The hospitalization was necessary primarily to adjust my doses due to my bipolar.

I had a bedroom window I used to stare out from, all kinds of thoughts racing through my mind.

During one of my hospitalizations, a nurse gifted me a small diary in which I could jot down all my thoughts and emotions, and even my kathak compositions. Here are some musings from it which continue to strike a chord within me and help me wrap up my reflections on my life as it has been lived so far.

*

I am surrounded by empty rooms.
Barricades for the mentally ill.
The situation couldn't be any worse.
People enter in and out, 'Beep!'
Key cards, key chains and hierarchy (of doctors, nurses, patients) seem to rule this universe,

Apart from legalized drugs which makes me question the legality of medical marijuana?

*

The night is too LONG for me to BELONG.
YESTERDAY doesn't exist;
Then why is it that we all want to dive deep within our pool of memories?
Aren't fresher, newer flowers better?
Instead of tossing the dead away, we can pay them respect.
Yes, he is non-existent for me NOW, this instant.
Does science hold the answers to all our questions?
Or is it religion, or even politics?
I think it's a medley of all things—all songs, dance and of course experimenting with life without burning my fingers...
I am in pursuit of universal truths,
Transcending my deepest, darkest, dancing desires.
That is the purpose of my writing.

*

The present reality is far from real; it is virtual, thanks to the age of electronics and isolation.
If we isolate ourselves, we will end up alone. [We know this. But] what we don't understand is [if] we are alone to begin with ... why the fear?
It's the fear of the unknown that crops up inside us.
It is important therefore we know,

But to know the unknown is impossible,
Once we know it is impossible, that is exactly where our strength will lie—knowing the inevitability of the unknown.

*

The stillness of the barks from my bedroom window,
Defines the random chaotic leaves that spring from its branches,
Their movement indicating the rhythmic speed of the breeze...
All this within the silence of my view.

*

Here is another short quote that I wrote in hospital: 'I have nothing to hide, I have nothing to fear ... I own my diamonds, and my dirt.' I am an open book—and that is indeed the approach I took to writing this memoir. I wanted the details of my experiences to positively impact people who were going through similar ordeals or who had witnessed it with friends or families. The second part of the quote is self-explanatory. All of us have flaws but when we really own them we will have the courage to correct them if needed. We wouldn't be lying to ourselves, especially about the kind of person we are, or strive to be.

*

A rather sensitive topic that I want to talk about pertains to one of my stays at the CAMH in Toronto. It was being debated whether or not I was ready for discharge. My doctor gave me the permission to go home but my mother was convinced that I needed to stay for a longer period to recover fully. I ended up having an argument with my mother that day. For a long time, I blamed her. But, time has provided a perspective to this too that wasn't there in that moment. I recall breaking down and crying in front of one of my favourite nurses who comforted me and convinced my mother that I was ready for home. That was the day my faith in the medical system was strengthened as I realized the mental health community offered a great deal of support to patients who needed it independent of any family opinions or preferences.

*

During my stay at the hospital, I often played music and danced my heart out in front of the phone camera. I still have those video recordings and although my rhythm and beats are all on time, my facial expressions are slightly different, which shows my sick state. Still in that madness, I strived for creativity and a way to channelize my high energy. Throughout my sickness I pursued my art and that is exactly what healed me, even more than the medicines. It is extremely important to try to keep in touch with any one aspect of yourself when you lose control of your mind to remind you of who you truly are. Trust me, when it is time to heal and return to your real self, you won't regret it.

Through torture and turmoil, you can always hug yourself to soothe the pain. Only when you start to love yourself can you receive it from others. Sometimes with help or guidance of a counsellor, friend or family member we can learn to love ourselves…

*

The post-pandemic period brought with it new beginnings in the form of the continuation of my bachelor's degree at George Brown College in Toronto. I became aware of a whole new world of early childhood education.

Children are the foundation for future generations. It is almost absurd that the role of an early childhood educator is reduced to simply that of a babysitter. It is our responsibility as a society to ensure that children are provided with an enriching environment wherein they learn to interact with their surroundings, peers, educators and families with ease. Today, in an environment where both parents go out to work, the maximum amount of time of a child's life is spent at a childcare centre. The seeds of many 'abnormalities' that may develop in the adult life of a child are sown in their early years. It is now known that the years from 0–6 are most crucial and can have grave positive or negative impacts in direct correlation with the quality of childcare. It is my desire that I work closely with young children to provide them with a healthy upbringing and create an appropriate learning environment that acts as a teacher along with the educators and the curriculum.

If we take tiny steps in the right direction at providing for and educating children at the same time, many changes can be made at the ground level without waiting for government intervention. We all need to take charge of prioritizing a child's early years on a daily basis. A child's well-being is the most important thing for the future. And it is never too early to start.

Research has shown that a negative foundation in early child education results in school failure, teen pregnancy, and criminality in an individual's second decade. In the third and fourth decades of life, the person is more at risk of obesity, depression, and elevated blood pressure. Premature aging can also occur as also memory loss. Thus, it is imperative that a child is provided with a strong foundation, and true progress on a larger scale towards this goal can only be made possible if the government actively participates in the early childhood education sector.

My area of interest is the mental health of children. I believe we can eliminate most mental health issues by focusing on the early years of a child and work from the position of preventing these disorders. Many triggers are in the environment, so it isn't merely the genes that act up. If we can work towards eliminating these triggers in the early stage of development, we can significantly reduce the number of mental health cases.

This will require the participation of families as much as children, and of course educators. It is in this field that I want to conduct research in, to find methods to reduce mental health issues by targeting the early years of a child and helping them make a smooth transition into adulthood.

Our lives are often an extension of our early childhood. I know this primarily because of my studies at George Brown. These early years, often beyond our control, make the biggest impact, positive or negative, on our adult lives. However, we must realize that as we grow older the onus of working on our personality is on us. Playing the blame game serves little purpose. The more we assume responsibility for our own success or mental health and well-being, the more agency we will have to make important life decisions for ourselves. It is tough to let go of memories of a bad childhood, but there are a few concepts such as self-regulation and resilience that we can aim to master. If you feel you have any such childhood memories or experiences that trouble you even in your adult life, it is advisable to talk about these feelings with a professional, a counsellor or doctor.

12

Living with Gratitude

Holding On and Letting Go

An Imaginary Conversation with my Therapist, Carrie, 2018

I was at my mother's studio in York University where I enacted this. We were doing a shoot for mum's film and we went to the York University campus studio. A 360-degree camera was being used, and my mother had placed some masks all over the room; the room was dark, and my mum directed me to walk, and wherever I went, they tried to follow me.

Later, as my emotions played out, my mum could see I had been through so much. She stopped me; she didn't want me to relive my dark memories. Here is the imaginary conversation I recorded:

Hi, Carrie. It's my birthday tomorrow. I just *had* to come see you, I have so much to tell you.

Okay, so I want to go to India this time; I miss him [my ex-boyfriend] so much, I have been moving from one place to another all my life. Obviously, it started in Mumbai where I was born. I don't think I can ever answer the question if someone asked me, 'Where are you from?' because I have lived in so many places, and I feel like I have been running away from each place. Like, I lived in Mumbai, but I hardly know most places in Mumbai; I just know the room where I grew up. And [now] it's broken down, completely broken down—there is a brand-new building…

Yeah, I know, places really aren't that important; it's the people that make the place. I have been trying to avoid places all my life.

You know I lived in Germany for a year, right? That was a rollercoaster! I think what defined me the most when I was in Germany was that I was an artist; and I always have been, I had this Facebook page, and I would have performances with my students and solo choreographies and post them on my page. Of course, no one was aware of the flip side of the coin. It was a huge thing, you know, it was my life actually. I labelled myself and I gave myself this name, 'Ishaa Tänzerin'. Tänzerin means 'dancer' in German, and Ishaa, of course, is my first name.

I had completed A1 level in German, and I wanted to be connected to the [local] people because you know how they always say, 'When in Rome, do as the Romans do.' [So] I was trying to fit in. But then, somehow I found that because of the identity crisis … like, I was there but still I was constantly questioning myself. Who was I? [I wondered.] Because when I was there, I would talk to so many people including a diverse range of immigrants—people from all walks of life. Like, my best friend, for example; she was from the continent of Africa—her name was Elsie. She's a mother; she tried to teach me everything that a good wife should do. She called me to her home one day and she laid [out] the table, and she told me, 'See, this is how you make the table and make your man happy!'

How do you make a man happy? And why should that be the purpose of anybody's life?

And then there are times where I question my upbringing. I think [I did this because] I want to be an early childhood educator [...] because that's what people do mostly, you know—whenever we learn anything, we connect our life and our own experiences [to it and try to make sense of what we have learned in that way]; and I thought the best way to learn about ECE (early childhood education) was indeed to use myself as a subject in my enquiries. How was I as an infant, a toddler and a school-goer?

And that's when I realized I hadn't seen that many baby pictures of myself, until recently [when] my mother showed me a black-and-white slideshow which she made for her film school (FTII) project [long ago]. It was the most beautiful experience for me to see all those photographs.

*

During the dark days of Covid, my beloved uncle Vir Papa passed away. It has been the greatest loss in my life. At first it seemed surreal, and I was in complete denial. I couldn't help feeling that if I still dialled his number, his voice would greet me at the other end. Perhaps I felt this because he had done so much and was always around, so I never associated the term 'unavailable' with him ever before.

But now I think that his loss was perhaps God's way of preparing me some more for life in general, with all its losses. This was the first real loss I had to deal with, but I knew that this was just the beginning. As melancholic as it may sound, it's true that eventually everyone will leave this world one by one and I will have to be as brave as I have been when I faced all that I have been through.

The experience of having lost my loved one reminded me again that everything I have been through, as much as I hated it sometimes, has brought me here, made me the strong woman I am today. And that's something to be proud of.

After all, despite having undergone several hospitalizations, being on various medications for more than a decade of my life, finding my way out of an abusive marriage, and constantly being moved across the globe, I am still dancing, studying and doing everything else I ever wanted to. I believe that all things happen for the best and what doesn't kill you only makes you stronger.

I know now that my resilience has been tested far too many times for it to fail now. I truly feel I can control my responses to almost any event now. As I have seen the worst, there really is nowhere left to go but forward—towards the *best* or, if that is too much to ask for, towards *better* times.

*

Analysing my past and attempting to interpret it, as I have done in this book, brings me to a set of reflections. I know that I am still fully capable of so many things, and it could have been a lot worse. I do not have any hallucinations anymore, and the only times I tend to fall sick is when I try to alter or stop my medication. While I am grateful for all this, I am grateful for one thing above all else: the illness that I once thought a demon is indeed a blessing. It's not that I never have moments when I ask why I had to have it, but there are many more moments now where I am grateful to have been diagnosed with such a disorder. It has brought me experiences and enriched my life in ways I could have never imagined.

I hope you too discover the power of disorder, and that there's something in my story that resonates with yours. But before you go, dear reader, tell me, now that you know everything about me—the good, the bad, and the ugly—can you find it in yourself to accept someone like me in your life, in your school, in your neighbourhood? As a friend? As your daughter? As your wife? As your beloved? Would you? Think, and you'll get to know yourself better than you ever did.

I would like to share with you, dear readers, to give hope to people coping with mental health issues that with perseverance and positivity, it is possible to have a fulfilling relationship fuelled by faith and a deep desire to love and commit. I met someone recently. His name is Biswarup Das. He is from India, a Bengali, and we recently got married, a life event that I thought I would never experience again. I do believe that love is indeed like a butterfly that comes and sits on your shoulder when you least expect it. It can never be forced.

When I confided in my father that I was about to marry, he told both my partner and me that instead of viewing each other as 'husband' and 'wife' as we most often do, we should look at each other as friends. That would help us sail successfully through any relationship.

A relationship is not a ready-made box of cookies you can pick up at the counter of a department store. You have to really knead that dough for just the right amount of time, and bake it to perfection. Then, of course, in order to consume the cookies, you have to make sure your stomach isn't bloated or too filled, and that you have enough hunger or desire to chew it till the very last crumb, and most importantly relish the flavour. Thankfully, I have my box of cookies, but I know at the end of the day or a few days they will be over, so I will have to get baking once again. It is a constant process. However, the amount of joy you take in the process equals the amount of satisfaction both you and your partner will receive as you savour the cookies.

Acknowledgements

I am grateful for my parents, Vinod and Shabnam, who would read each draft without judgement and provide positive feedback. I've also reached a place in life where I'm thankful for my bipolar disorder. Without this imbalance in my life, I wouldn't seek to find order in disorder.

I would like to give special thanks to Anu-mummy, who gave me the idea of writing a memoir on my experiences with bipolar. Next up is Ishan, my brother, for being such a strong source of support throughout my writing process. My brother Agni, who would read my drafts and give me his inputs which were much appreciated. My sister Zuni, for being such a great source of inspiration through her writings and her academics at Stanford. For my sisters, Ananya and Saumya, for demonstrating sheer strength and positivity through rough times. I can never be thankful enough to my aunt, Shelly Bua, for her support and sound advice throughout my life. She has always been a role model for me, especially as she brings the family together and acts as a binding factor, while also being a mother figure for all of us.

I am thankful to Abba, my stepfather, for always having been a pillar of emotional support for me, and providing me with immense love and care, no matter what. Also, I am eternally grateful for his objective opinions on my life.

During my hospitalizations, I needed companionship the most. The people who stayed committed to our friendship were true friends indeed. Several people stopped talking to me after my illness, and yet there were a few, who stayed by my side and even visited me in hospitals. Sara Rasikh and Sidhant Sharma were a great support; I would call them ever so often complaining about my life in the hospital. Sometimes, I wasn't even coherent due to the illness and the medications, but they still listened. Hence, I feel that going through a tough time is a blessing in disguise, for you will always find your true friends by your side, against all odds.

I would like to take this opportunity to talk a little bit about the friendships that I have formed over the years. It is extremely challenging to make and sustain friendships; however, the ones I do make tend to stay with me forever.

My friend Shinchana Chakraborty has always been there for me in my toughest moments. Tanvi Shashikant is a friend from my boarding school days and she knows me inside out—my flaws and my strengths. They never judge my illness or ever have anything negative to say about me; rather, they push me in the right direction by pointing out the pros and cons of any situation without being pessimistic.

During my time in Germany, I made friends with Sonya Moses, Elsie Avril, Fatema Darbar and Isha Rakheja. I haven't been able to keep in touch with them, but I have extremely fond memories of them and will never forget their support and advice through the rough times I faced in my personal life back then. Veit Kuehne was yet another strong source of support I had, especially because of his large gatherings of students and immigrants.

Here in Toronto, my friends Cayte Kim and Shizu Yamaguchi have always had my back.

All my friends, who have supported me, just like my family. And especially my late uncle, Vir papa, who would always be open to hearing my side of the story and would be more than willing to offer advice when I needed it—the world's best advice.

Thanks to Dr Guru Dhillon and Mrs Annu Dhillon for providing me with the serene work environment I had in Dalhousie Public School; it was much needed for me to write this book.

I am grateful to my nani (maternal grandma), Kanta Sukhdev, for giving me the strength to cope with my mental health condition, providing a living example of how to deal with hardships and the sheer strength of a woman.

I would especially like to thank Anju Christine Lingham, a dear friend who helped reorganize and edit the initial draft of my book, and Soumitra Ranade who introduced me to Anju.

I am ever so grateful to my editor, Shantanu Ray Chaudhuri, for having faith in the sensitive themes explored in this book and for so gracefully accepting my story and bringing it to the world. Having had an overlapping view of mental health it was in both our interests to advocate for and engage in conversations around it. A word of thanks also for Purnima Bhattacharya for going through the final proofs with a fine-toothed comb.

Special thanks to Amitabh Gupta ji, who worked tirelessly with Shantanu and me to ensure that nothing in the text hurt anyone. Memories are tricky and need empathetic people to make sense of them. I was lucky to have the support and advice of Amitabh and Shantanu in this emotionally charged project.

Special thanks and hugs to Anuja Singh, who helped in the final process of editing and provided a newer, fresher perspective on the memoir.

And last, but not least, thank you Bhagwan-ji for everything. I am grateful for most of my life experiences without which I wouldn't have evolved to become the person I am today. So, thank you, God, for giving me the chance to improve myself and learn from my experiences.

In Gratitude

Dr Rajesh Parikh
Dr Parul Doshi: Counsellor
Dr Soumitra Pathare
Dr Nilesh Shah
Dr Suparna Telang
Dr Yusuf Merchant (who passed away recently)
Dr Gary Sachs
Peta-Gaye Ebanks: Academic Counsellor and Life Coach (Toronto, Canada)
Guru Pta Maneesha Sathe: Kathak Guru
Guru Shubhada Varadkar: Odissi Guru
Ewa-Maria Cherukuru: Latin Ballroom Teacher
Vinay Murgod: Football and Life Coach (UPSA, Pune, India)
The Yoga Institute, Mumbai
Dr David Nahirney (Edmonton, AB, Canada)
Dr Shari Swartz (SHN Network, Toronto, Canada)
Dr Adam Tasca
CAMH (Toronto, Canada)
Sunnybrook Hospital, Toronto, Canada

George Brown College: School of Early Childhood
Dr (Capt.) G.S. Dhillon: Chairman, Dalhousie Public School
Sahyadri School
Vernon Barford Junior High School (Edmonton, AB)
Harry Ainlay High School (Edmonton, AB)
Symbiosis College of Arts and Commerce (Pune, India)
Bharati Vidyapeeth Deemed University (Pune, India)